HELP!
MY KID HATES
WRITING

ALSO BY JULIE BOGART

The Brave Learner
Raising Critical Thinkers
Becoming a Critical Thinker

HELP!
MY KID HATES WRITING

IIIIIIIIIIIIIIIIIIIIIIIIIIIIIIIII

HOW TO TURN STRUGGLING
STUDENTS INTO BRAVE WRITERS

IIIIIIIIIIIIIIIIIIIIIIIIIIIIIIIII

JULIE BOGART

A TarcherPerigee Book

tarcherperigee

an imprint of Penguin Random House LLC
1745 Broadway, New York, NY 10019
penguinrandomhouse.com

TarcherPerigee with tp colophon is a registered trademark of Penguin Random House LLC

Book design by Angie Boutin

Library of Congress Cataloging-in-Publication Data

Names: Bogart, Julie, 1961- author.
Title: Help! My kid hates writing: how to turn struggling students into brave writers / Julie Bogart.
Description: New York: TarcherPerigee, 2025 | Includes bibliographical references and index.
Identifiers: LCCN 2024033342 (print) | LCCN 2024033343 (ebook) |
  ISBN 9780593713167 (hardcover) | ISBN 9780593713174 (epub)
Subjects: LCSH: Composition (Language arts)—Study and teaching. | Creative writing—Study and teaching. | English language—Composition and exercises—Study and teaching. | Artificial intelligence—Educational applications.
Classification: LCC LB1575.8.B64 2025 (print) | LCC LB1575.8 (ebook) |
  DDC 372.62/3044—dc23/eng/20250116
LC record available at https://lccn.loc.gov/2024033342
LC ebook record available at https://lccn.loc.gov/2024033343

Printed in the United States of America
1st Printing

The authorized representative in the EU for product safety and compliance is Penguin Random House Ireland, Morrison Chambers, 32 Nassau Street, Dublin D02 YH68, Ireland, https://eu-contact.penguin.ie.

To Cindy Clark, Dawn Smith, and Kirsten Merryman—
brave thinkers, writers, and collaborators. My bottomless
gratitude for the gift of each of you in my life and work.

To my mother, Karen O'Connor, my first and best writing teacher,
who passed away right as this book went to press. I love you, Mom.

Everyone with a native language has what it takes to write well and punctuate adequately.

—PETER ELBOW

CONTENTS

||||||||||||||||||||||||||||

||||||||||||||||||||||||||||||||

How Writing Makes Cowards of Us All

Writing scares the living daylights out of, well, just about everyone at some point in their life. Ever sent a text and wanted to take it back, immediately? I have. I hate that. I've lost sleep in terror that a bold statement I posted online would come back to bite me in the tush when a superior thinker destroyed my argument publicly. Worse, what if that critic notices my *its* and *it's* are mixed up, not because I don't know better but because my mind, on fire with a virtuous cause, is making a case for my argument faster than my editing brain can keep pace? Does this happen to you too? I knew it.

When the internet was new, my peer group was shocked to discover that the people we thought we knew and liked were, sadly, blockheads. Their writing betrayed them. We had access to their innermost thoughts, and many times, we didn't like what we found. Suddenly, we all wanted to set each other straight. You can't believe the online bloodbaths I witnessed between stay-at-home moms, for instance. They insulted each other over which loving, devoted mother was ruining the planet faster: Pampers parents or cloth-diaper-service subscribers. This was a real debate that led to brutal written attacks. The keyboard warrior was born! In other words, my generation invented trolling—you're welcome.

What about you? Maybe you screwed up your courage to write a note to your crush in seventh grade: "Do you like me? Check Yes or No." Maybe you turned in a college paper confident you did a great job, only to earn a disheartening B– for no clear reason. Maybe you're haunted by a vague fear that someone will discover you don't know how many *c*'s and *m*'s are in the word *accommodate* (guilty!). When we speak, we get to say "Um" and "That's not what I meant" and "Sorry, let me try again." But put what you think in writing, and look out! You're on the hook for perfect accuracy—from spelling to facts to grammar.

Today, the stakes for writing are both lower and higher than ever. They're lower because we live in a glut of writing. Everyone can write and be published (all hail the glorious internet). Whether you post comments on a news website, compose fan fiction, or write a horticulture Substack with tips for tending ornamentals, readers who share your interests will find and read your writing. You don't need an agent or traditional publisher to get your words to the marketplace. In fact, in the twenty-first century, more human beings are writing for publication (readers) than in the history of the world. Cue choirs of angels!

On the flip side, the stakes for writing are higher than ever before. Yes, you can reach an audience easily, but for the first time in history, you'll also get that audience's immediate reaction to what they think about your qualifications to write about that topic. Everyone is a smug critic of grammar, spelling, punctuation, opinions, and ideas. Public writing sometimes feels like drunken ax-throwing—self-righteous, ill-prepared taunts get flung at the writer, followed by piling on in the form of likes and comments from the crowd. Even bad writers are self-appointed critics of other people's better writing! It's infuriating.

And don't get me started on AI! Or—do get me started. What's to be done about artificial intelligence whipping up a complete draft of my ideas in seconds, typing the words in real time in front of my eyes, applying the correct formatting with nary a grammatical error before I finish my cup of tea? It's nearly impossible to "resist the assist" for many of today's writing tasks—it would be like saying no to calculators or Photoshop. There's no going back either. Remember when electricity took the world by storm? Lamplighters were destined to lose their livelihoods no matter how much we romanticized candles over light bulbs.

Maybe we're at the end of an era. Is the physical act of writing our own thoughts destined for the waste bin of history? Today, like Elle Woods from *Legally Blonde*, many of our students will create video essays for their college applications instead of writing them. Will AI take over texting, emailing, and online game chatting too? Is poetry to be written by robots? Will TV shows, movies, plays, and novels use artificial intelligence to steal writing styles from successful authors rather than hire *people* to do the job?

Never in our history have we successfully built a tool that is *creative* in the way humans are. Is that what's happening here? Honestly, it's refreshing to see how alarmed everyone is. It shows we *value* the combination of writing and humanity!

We're literally saying: "The thoughts in my head *have to be* and *are* more valuable than what a computer can generate."

Still, every educator and parent ought to be asking: "Why in the h-e-double-toothpicks *should* our kids learn to write from scratch when they resent it so much and artificial intelligence can do it for them?" I mean, really! Children and teens tell us all the time how much they hate writing and that they don't have anything worthwhile to put on the page. These are the wordy protestations of children who can't manage to jot a thank-you note to Grandma for the slick new dirt bike she gave as a birthday gift.

Adults resent writing too! I hear from them all the time. They send me emails quaking in fear that I'm about to judge them for a typo or missed punctuation mark. (I would never! But they don't know that.) Maybe we need to start by asking ourselves: "Why should we, as parents and educators, bother with the drama and trauma of teaching the art of transcription (jotting down our own thoughts by our own hands) when so many human beings are resistant to the physical act of putting pen to paper, video is everywhere, and AI is on the move?" Great question.

For many grown-ups, these swift changes feel like the end of an era. We romanticize letters written in someone's identifiable penmanship. If you're the family historian who relishes the artifacts of your lineage, you grieve twice. The handwritten journals, photographs, and letters of today are rarely saved in a shoebox. Instead, most of our writing and photography is stored in pixels. As technologies evolve, many of those legacies are being rapidly lost through digital decay. Historians share this sense of loss. Despair for the old paper, parchment, or cave wall ways of writing is real.

Or maybe you're secretly fist pumping in joy! You've been waiting for the end of original writing as a requirement all your life. Digital records are easy to keep and to edit. You've got the support of grammar and spell check. You won't be judged by the grammar snobs. You can stop feeling guilty that you never write thank-you notes, because now you can punch out a text message in thirty seconds flat—or dictate it voice-to-text in even less time. You wonder if you can quit writing from scratch for good and let artificial intelligence do it all. Hurray: writing is over!

Let's take a deep collective breath. Whether you have nostalgia for paper-and-pen writing or are relieved that today's technologies have made self-expression easier, the art of writing isn't going anywhere. Original thought can never be reproduced by a machine. Our deepest sentiments, the joy we find in self-expression, our particular take on an issue—these lie within us and can't be imitated or discovered by artificial intelligence. Not only that, original writing is still the best tool for education (that is, developing as a thinker) and is essential in all kinds of careers. Just because AI can generate raw copy doesn't mean that it can tell the stories in *your child's* imagination or analyze the meaning of texts the way they strike *your teenager.*

Consider this era the dawn of truly remarkable breakthroughs in writing. Will there be liabilities and doomsday predictions about the end of civilization? Yes. Most reasonable people are worried about plagiarism, copyright violations, and students not turning in their own written work. But even college students in the 1950s, armed with mere fountain pens, paid their roommates to write their history papers. (A career lawyer I know confessed to this very practice. Mind blown!)

Where there's a will not to write from scratch, there's always been a way.

The difference today is that we can opt out of writing (and thinking!) more easily than ever. Since that is the case, the question before us really is: *Why write?* The answer can't be to get into college, to hold a job, or to prove to Grandma that you understand the rules of etiquette. The importance of writing is more fundamental. Why did people make intentional, meaningful markings on the cave walls of Lascaux, France, seventeen thousand years ago? Why have human beings created entire alphabets and symbolic systems to convey their thoughts? Why are we swept into delirium at the sight of the Beast's library when he shows it to Belle?

There's a reason, and it's pretty simple, actually. Human beings are communicators at their core. They want to know each other. Writing invites us inside someone else's mind and preserves those thoughts—humans find that experience irresistible. With one voice, writers declare: "What I have to say is worth safeguarding and reading." And readers everywhere say: "Thank you. I wanted to know!"

It's this primal impulse to get our thought lives out into the sunshine that makes writing vibrate with power. We write to know ourselves, and we read to know one another. Language itself is fantastical—it evokes a host of pleasures from emotion to insight to perspective. We are drawn in by its sounds and called forward by the way it connects us to one another.

Weirdly, your kids already understand this principle even before they learn to read. Have you ever heard a small child get into a rhyming riot, where they string together as many rhyming words as they can, even inventing new ones just to keep the scheme going? *Giggle, wiggle, piggle, biggle, fliggle, triggle, jiggle, besmiggle!* The playfulness of the words, the sounds, the body sensations are all a part of the utter fascination that is the birthright of every human being. We love wordplay, communication, and the call and response of language. Put those words on paper and look out! Kids already know that writing means: *My thoughts, in those markings, matter.* A writer has a transcendent experience: *There I am, outside of my skin, on a surface, shared with readers.*

Here's my bold claim: *Writing is for writers first, readers second.*

I'm reminded of a powerful moment early in my writing-instruction career. A ten-year-old student in one of our Brave Writer writing classes, whom I'll call Gary, had a rare disease that required daily growth hormones. Every day, the boy's father injected an extremely painful shot into his stomach. Gary's mother told the instructor that her son *hated* the shot and that she felt utterly unable to help him process this traumatic, necessary experience that went on day after day.

In our classes, we teach students how to freewrite—how to let the thoughts in your mind flow down through your arm so the words pour out of your hand onto the page. The only rule: keep the pencil moving. We suggest the parent guide the child by telling them that they can write whatever comes to mind, even if it seems like the wrong thing to say. For instance, some kids will write, "I hate this. When can I stop writing?" We say: "Yes, that counts!" And so, this sweet boy took his mother's instructions to heart and did just that—Gary wrote his real thoughts, without regard to spelling, punctuation, grammar, or even worrying about who might read his writing.

The first line of Gary's first freewrite attacked his father with an expletive and accused him of hating all children. Gary's rage spilled all over the page unedited, the way it lived inside of him. His caring mother held space for this hard-to-read journey as her son wrote three times in a period of days on the same topic: how much he hated the injections delivered by his father.

In his third freewrite, however, Gary softened. He began with this line: "My dad is usually a nice guy, but at the point when he was giving me the shot, I felt like he was someone who liked giving kids pain." Note the way Gary's perspective expanded and became less self-oriented after he gave himself permission to express a private forbidden thought first. There's research that shows that writing four freewrites of fifteen minutes each over the course of four days about a distressing or traumatic event will provide an enormous amount of healing to the writer—on par with therapy! It was incredible to see this exact process in action in our classes.

This is one of the powerful reasons human beings write, and it's why helping children learn to do it themselves is both a moral obligation and a privilege. Writing lets us externalize what's inside, putting it into language, making it a "thing out there" rather than a complicated, hidden "thing in here." We get off track quickly if we teach writing as a performance for teachers or to impress readers. From where I sit, we write not just to convey an idea to another person (which is an important goal), but first to know and value our own thoughts and experiences.

The only person in the entire world who thinks your thoughts is *you*. In school, kids miss that memo. They think the thoughts they're supposed to write live in the teacher's mind or in a book they should emulate (or inside ChatGPT). Yet when a person realizes the amazing capacity their brain has to generate ideas, insights, descriptions, stories, and analyses, writing takes on an entirely different dimension! It becomes important personally. I like to say about my company, Brave Writer, that we teach *writers*, not *writing*. The human being is the conduit of written language—not the assignment, not the information, not even the proper mechanics. Artificial intelligence can never provide the moving, rings-true content that a specific human being can. Until our kids understand that the ideas that live in them are valuable and unique, writing will continue to be a source of irritation and black magic—an incantation they need to conjure to sound "right" to the teacher-reader, rather than be true to the self.

People who write for a living (academics, novelists, journalists, researchers, memoirists, physicists, and more) agree that writing clarifies thinking in ways thought alone never can. I can think an amazing thought in the shower that falls to pieces when I towel off and start typing it onto a screen. Every time, writing shows me what I don't quite understand well enough yet. But writing also shows me what I am afraid to face or reveal. Sometimes writing shows me something I didn't think until the moment my hand made the move. Writing is a means for externalizing the self. In putting that self at arm's length (quite literally—the distance of an arm to a page or screen), we get a different view of ourselves. As my writing mentor, Dr. Peter Elbow, says: "Writing helps us stand outside ourselves."

A reason to raise writers is so that our kids have the sheer joy of standing outside themselves to know their minds, their feelings, and their experiences with a little critical distance. When they write, they give value and weight to the essence of who they are. In the last thirty years of online communication, it's become obvious to me that kids love to write for that very reason! They'll sneak a cell phone to bed so they can text all night long. They happily type into a chat for hours while gaming. They design social media pages, and before that, they created online diaries, emptying their hearts to that imagined audience of peers. They write scripts for short videos and podcasts. In truth, they can think of no better way to spend their time. They see writing as a tool for both self-expression *and* powerful communication with readers/viewers/listeners they value. From the moment the internet threw open its doors, kids everywhere clamored for a space to fill with their passions, interests, and curiosities—and they used writing to do it!

Of course, most kids balk at the kind of writing school requires. Let's be real. Only "nerds" get excited about writing a compare-and-contrast essay for a single reader (a teacher) who's going to mark it up, note all its flaws, and then assign it a grade. What an awful system for learning to write. It's like learning to play the piano simply so a teacher can tell you all the notes you missed while no one else gets to enjoy the music you make.

The point of this book, then, is to strengthen your young writers so that writing becomes meaningful to them in the following ways:

* They know themselves better.

* They clarify and expand their thinking.

* They delight in language.

* They communicate effectively with readers.

* They face a blank page or screen with confidence.

* They perform writing tasks for school and their careers with competence.

* They discover the power of writing for themselves, beyond school settings.

* They write that thank-you note to Grandma!

Many adults have bad memories of writing in school. You may discover as you read this book that you're healing the damaged writer that lives in you too. I've spoken to thousands of adults at conferences for three decades. It's startling to see how many grown-ups (by my guesstimate, a good 75 to 80 percent) still feel intimidated by writing, even after twelve, sixteen, eighteen years of schooling. The education establishment is not doing a good job of releasing the writers within us. We feel tethered to the performance metrics of school and never quite shed them.

Unfortunately, the way writing is usually taught to kids creates untold stress and even, yes, damage. We'll look at how that damage gets created and what to do to both heal and prevent it going forward. In fact, it's pretty easy to throw off the weight of all that critique once you have a better sense of how the writing journey can unfold for your kids and for you!

By the way, I'm not here to give you an academic peer-reviewed study of how kids learn to write in school. Dozens of articles online tell that story. Rather, I want to share with you what happens when we treat children as wise, capable, and insightful people *while* teaching them to write. I put their raw emotions and delightful idiosyncrasies at the center of my writing pedagogy. The students I want to help are children—those playful, precocious, quirky beings who become the stars of every conversation because their way of speaking and thinking is so wildly original. These are kids of parents and caregivers—adults—who want to create the best conditions for their children to become not only competent writers and thinkers but also, eventually, grown-ups who can face a blank screen without having a panic attack.

Wouldn't it be beautiful if your kids knew how to use writing to clarify their own thoughts or to persuade a resistant audience? Someday they may want to write their own wedding vows or journal when they have troubling thoughts. Let's give them that gift! Once they know writing is within their power, the writing tasks for school become much easier to tackle too.

This book is divided into twelve chapters. Each chapter addresses an aspect of what it means to grow as a writer. What sets this book apart from a writing curriculum is that it teaches you, the adult, about your crucial role in that journey.

YOUR WRITING ASSIGNMENT

You didn't think I was going to ask you to write? Think again. This is a writing book so, yes, you'll be writing too. Grab something to write on, whether it's a pretty journal, a sheet of scrap paper, or a Word document on your computer. This will be your writing notebook as you do the assignments at the end of each chapter in this book. Jot down a few of your thoughts and memories about writing (even single words will do). What feelings come up when you think of writing, teaching writing, or even just helping your child with writing homework? You might even scribble a few feeling words in the margin of this book.

||||||||||||||||||||

CHAPTER 1

Writing Is Hard

L et's get down to brass tacks. Writing is hard.

There. I said it.

Before we continue, however, I want to understand how you heard the word *writing* in that context. What kind of writing popped into your mind when you read "Writing is hard"? Did you picture handwriting? That's usually what feels difficult to a five-year-old. Maybe you remembered your uncertainty about semicolons and your most commonly misspelled words. For kids ages eight to ten, writing often means learning to spell and punctuate accurately. Did your mind flash back to corrections on a paper? Middle schoolers hear the word *writing* and likely picture composition of some kind—a limerick, a report, a letter, a descriptive paragraph. By high school, a student thinks writing means crafting an essay or a research paper. You may be remembering the sting of receiving a lower grade than you expected or reading a teacher's vague, cryptic margin notes that did nothing to help you improve the next paper. Writing *is* hard.

I've gotten into many debates about what constitutes the true definition of writing. Reading specialists are particularly interested in training handwriting skills for letter formation, spelling, and reading fluency. Academic writing teachers prioritize the formats most commonly used in school. Writing courses for would-be authors focus on developing one's writing voice and connecting to readers with the goal of selling articles and books to publishers. These many different aspects of putting text to paper or screen make the act of teaching writing complex. Writers manage multiple systems in their minds and hands all at once while monitoring their very real thoughts as they transcribe them.

Will the *real* definition of writing please stand? In fact, each of these aspects of writing matters, and we'll look at all of them in this book. That said, I won't address how to teach reading; reading is its own skill. And if you're worried about spelling and how to correctly use an em dash, we'll get there. Promise! But first, let's start at the very beginning.

BECOMING AN AUTHOR

Back when my oldest son, Noah, was twelve months old, he sat in a high chair behind me while I hand-washed our lunch dishes. "Nana," he called—surprising me, since this was the first intelligible word I had ever heard him say. I wheeled around and repeated the word: "Nana?" And then, as a conscientious mother who loves all things language, I launched into a little speech:

Noah, you said "nana." Did you know that's part of a word? The word is "banana." It's a noun! You can use it in a sentence like this: "I would like a banana." Because you are making a request, you want to use that noun within the oral format called "etiquette." So you would say, "Mama, I would like a banana, please."

Okay, did I really say all that to my baby boy? I did not! Which you probably already knew, because no adult in their right mind corrects a babbling baby who is learning to talk.

Here's what I actually did. I immediately called to Noah's father to come downstairs. We fed Noah banana slices trying to get him to say the word again. We retired the word *banana* from our vocabulary and only used Noah's term, *nana*. I made an international phone call to my mother to celebrate. And then I did what every new mother of a firstborn does: I wrote Noah's first word in his baby book, dating it as a written record of his oral speech, so that readers for decades to come would enjoy reading Noah's first attempt at speech: "nana." In short, I turned him into an author.

An author is a person whose thought world has been committed to paper, a screen, or another written format for readers to consume. Some authors type or handwrite their own words, but that is by no means a requirement for being an author. People with particular disabilities (everything from dyslexia to paralysis to missing limbs) rely heavily on transcription services in order to convey their ideas in writing. At Brave Writer, we have two teachers whose physical limitations prevent them from typing; they rely on Dragon voice-to-text software to compose their responses to students, speaking their comments into a laptop microphone to write. The author of the beautiful book *The Diving Bell and the Butterfly*, Jean-Dominique Bauby, was completely paralyzed except for the use of one eye. He wrote his entire memoir by blinking!

In the 1980s, a friend of mine who'd been diagnosed with dyslexia as a child grew weary of the way his spelling limitations created drag when he was doing the hard work of thinking and analyzing. So he composed his PhD thesis orally into a small Dictaphone recording device and paid a secretarial service to transcribe it. My question to you: Who got the PhD? The secretary with perfect spelling and punctuation? Or my friend, the doctoral candidate? Naturally, my friend did. No one on the doctoral candidacy committee disqualified him because he didn't demonstrate his own perfect spelling or typing skills. Rather, his ideas were the priority.

The point is: Any person who can externalize thought and find a method for putting that thought into written transcription is a writer. Any writer who is read is an author. A bold declaration, but I stand by it!

Once you believe that a writer lives inside your child's body already and is simply in need of a transcription mechanism, you'll get your priorities straight. The mistake we've made in education is similar to the absurd little speech I pretended to make to Noah as he learned to speak. We snuff the liveliness out of our children's writing by our relentless need to correct and contain a child's unruly self-expression and not-yet-fluent mechanics. When we do, we disincentivize the risk-taking behavior necessary for a writer to flourish! Let's teach the mechanics of writing, yes, but not at the expense of children's unbridled natural impulse to share the thoughts and ideas most meaningful to them. We also want to embrace the messy, stop-and-start journey of learning to put all those thoughts into accurate prose.

Handwriting, typing, spelling, and punctuation are all *transcription* skills—how to take dictation from your own mind. When I talk about writing, I'm referring to a person's thought life: the ideas that live inside that agile, brilliant child-mind. Writing begins with speech—getting those thoughts and ideas out of our bodies and brains. Talking lets us experiment, backtrack, restate, and refine our thoughts. Writing structures those thoughts. When you write what you think, the words you put on the page or screen feel more important and permanent than speech. Have you noticed an uptick in anxiety when you have to read your own writing to an audience? How much truer is that for a child? In order for kids to learn to write, then, the environment must be as emotionally supportive and free as it is for speech. Reread that sentence. We want to coax young writers to take writing risks the same way we egged them on to try new words or phrases as toddlers.

Once Noah used the word *nana*, his dad and I happily adopted that word instead of *banana* for months. We didn't worry that our child would never learn the correct term. We found ourselves mimicking Noah *and also* speaking accurately to him: we used both versions of the word naturally, unself-consciously. We trusted a process that required our confidence and mirroring. Over time, Noah took new risks: "Mama, my want nana." This grammatically awkward sentence still effectively communicated what he wanted us to know. We were thrilled! Both parents appreciated and encouraged his fledgling speaker skills.

Sometimes I would say back to Noah in a gentle, playful tone: "Do you mean to say, 'I want a banana'?" I'd wait to see if he'd try to imitate me. Whatever the result, I gave him bananas. As he gained fluency in speech, he became more precise. He imitated us, his parents, and made wild guesses that had some correspondence to the patterns his mind was adopting for speech. He might say "goed" instead of "went" or "her" instead of "she." When he declared that he wanted "waterlemon" instead of "watermelon," we found it so adorable we copied that malaprop into his baby book. To this day, we jokingly refer to watermelons as "waterlemons," even though Noah is thirty-seven years old. Our family celebrated every bit of communication with utter confidence that Noah would eventually be a fluent, competent speaker. We were at ease. We trusted the process. We participated in it.

There were times we gave him a script: "Say 'thank you' to your auntie!" We didn't wonder if he was plagiarizing us. We wanted him to master the patterns of fluent English. By five years old, most first-language speakers are brilliantly comfortable in their family's heart language. They know syntax, verb conjugations, and a sizable vocabulary—and they speak all of those words with a flawless local accent.

One day, when Noah was five years old, he shouted to me from the other room with complete ease: "Hey, Mama! Get me a banana!" Now that Noah had this level of fluency, I shouted back to him, "Hey! What do you say?" Because Noah could speak without thinking about talking, I could expect him to apply the convention called etiquette to his speech without it causing him to stumble. He could add the word *please* to his request. Noah wasn't ready to give oral reports or lead a board meeting, but he could be guided to the ways we organize oral language to be polite. Over time, he would learn other oral formats like reciting a poem, narrating the storyline of a book we read together, giving a presentation, or going on a job interview. Each one was taught when he was skillful enough in speaking to manage it.

I'm making a case for a similar approach in writing. Do we put a child's early attempts at spelling in the baby book the way I did with "nana"? We should! "Sellabrashun" is adorable and built from the phonetics the child knows—but do we see it that way? Or do we shudder and worry that if the child misspells *celebration*, it'll stick? Do we notice the energy of what the child risked putting on the page or only that the handwriting looks "sloppy"? Do we save advanced formats for when the child's mechanics in writing are automatic and fluent, or do we expect perfect spelling and punctuation from a nine-year-old, and for all the sentences to be logically organized into an essay too?

The brain is hardwired for speech. It takes about five years to become a fluent native speaker of any language simply through immersion, the attentive mirroring of a caregiver, and gentle guidance to correct minor mistakes in usage (barring a language impairment). Reading and writing are secondary skills that must be taught and learned once a child speaks easily. In looking at the research about writing proficiency, most would agree that it takes about ten years to go from not reading and writing at all to having proficient handwriting, spelling, punctuation, organization, and application of academic writing formats.

Most kids don't begin putting their original thoughts into writing in their own hand until they're about eight years old (though the first attempts at writing sentences usually coordinate with fluency in reading and handwriting, so this age may vary child to child). When someone says to me that their eight-year-old is a terrible speller, I remind them, "Of course they are! They're like a one-year-old saying their first words."

That means your kids have from about eight until eighteen to grow those practical writing skills. A twelve-year-old is only halfway through that timeline and will likely still make a notable number of spelling and punctuation errors as a result. But just because the mechanics take time to master doesn't mean that we ignore the most vital part of anyone's writing— their lively thought life! What if we limited our children to speaking only when they could perform the English language without errors? They'd hate to talk, that's what!

No matter what you think writing instruction ought to entail, it's not even necessarily essential that your kids learn to "write." You read that right. Earlier in this chapter, I talked about authors who don't have the physical ability to transcribe their own thoughts. Does that mean they can't be writers? No— it means they can't be their own transcriptionists, the secretaries of their mind's thoughts. The mechanics of writing (like handwriting, typing, spelling, and punctuation) are servants of written self-expression. These skills can be performed by the one composing the thoughts, or by someone for hire, or by the magic of voice-to-text software. Those who can't handwrite or type aren't barred from having a life as a writer. Content is what drives writing, not mechanics. The mechanics of writing merely convey the content—not the other way around.

Nevertheless, most kids will have the chance to learn to write using their own minds *and* hands. It's this mix of handwriting or typing while thinking original thoughts that leads to the experience kids report: that writing is hard! The rise in high school and university students using programs like Chat-GPT is sending a clear message: writing from scratch feels daunting. How do we balance learning the mechanics of writing against the sophisticated wordiness of original thinking? After all, writing is the exposing of a self, in a quasi-permanent form, all while applying a bunch of "rules" correctly. Kids know this intuitively. Adults forget it regularly.

I want to get one thing straight as we wade into the rapids of writing instruction. This book champions the cause of children. Too many children declare: "I hate writing." Too many adults respond: "You can't mean that." I believe kids when they tell me that they hate writing—that it's boring, that they don't see the point, that their hands hurt, that there are too many rules, and that revision feels pointless. Some kids are adamant that they'll *never* use writing once they grow up to be a video-game tester, so why learn it now? Others dramatically declare that they can't think of anything to write, even though five minutes before they yakked a parent's ear off with all the things they had to say.

You may notice some of these behaviors when you encourage your kids to write:

* They fidget.

* They cry.

* They slide off the chair.

* They stare blankly into space.

* They dissolve into a fit of giggles or tears.

One mother told me that her child tested her by writing the word "poop" sixteen times in a row to fill up the three lines required for the homework assignment. Even many kids who like writing for pleasure still don't like writing for school. They want to write stories for people to purchase and read, not crank out a tedious "descriptive paragraph of a dirt clod" (a real assignment in one curriculum I reviewed). When they share their writing—the kind they write for fun—too often the adult cringes over a misspelling or missing capital letter. The child's feelings are hurt. The child decides: *Why take that risk again?*

Kids are honest, but sometimes we treat their honesty like an inconvenience or, at the extreme, like they're lying. We say unhelpful stuff like "Everyone has to do things they don't like" or "When you're thirty-six and married with two kids, you'll have to know how to write. Now get going!" The eight-year-old hasn't yet lived a decade, but sure! Let's expect them to imagine being full-grown grumpy adults like us. What if we took their declarations seriously? What *do* kids hate about writing, exactly? Are they saying that they don't like thinking thoughts, or are they pointing to some other aspect of the writing process that creates this emotional drag?

To declare, "I hate writing" is to say, "I hate my thoughts." Yet that's not what we think we're saying when we say we hate writing. Most people are rejecting a system of evaluation that destroys confidence in self-expression—which *is* why many kids (and adults!) hate writing. It's painful to be told that what you offered of yourself falls short of an academic standard. If the goal of a writing assignment is to magically guess what the teacher has in mind, why wouldn't a student be tempted to let artificial intelligence take a stab at writing that paper?

I have often asked myself why the school system hasn't reinvented writing instruction, given the deplorable results. I'm not saying everyone has to *love* writing. I'd settle for not hating it. It would be amazing if the goal were to teach kids to feel confident and competent when called on to write, wouldn't it? It would be wonderful if kids knew that their thoughts were more important and insightful than what a chatbot could generate. But because school is designed for graded, standardized progress, the old methods continue. Messy freedom is not welcome for long in most classrooms.

WHY WRITING IS "HARD"

Writing depends on the combination of three skill sets that grow at different rates.

1. Reading: the ability to decode, spell, and punctuate accurately
2. Transcription: the ability to make the letters with your own hands through handwriting or typing
3. Composition: the ability to order thoughts in an appropriate structure

Ironically, the skill called "composition" is the one most kids develop first. Sure, they aren't speaking in eloquent essays or performing speeches. But they have a good sense of self-expression. They know how to make their thoughts known through speech. They can retell a personal experience or explain why their sibling is to blame for waking the baby. They can ask for what they need or want (more time on the iPad!). They can organize a process into steps. They're able to emphatically state why they hate rainbow sprinkle pancakes with their own set of reasons. Even children who are quieter or have some language delays are busy internalizing the structures of speech, through listening and through their attempts to participate.

Too often, educators treat writing like it's a completely different language than the one kids know well. In fact, in many writing programs that I've reviewed, the thesis *is* that learning to write is like learning another language. We'll talk more about that in a minute, but I want you to sit with how odd that feels to hear. By five years old, you're fluent in speech. Yet those very thoughts and words you know how to express with ease are somehow unrelated to the words and thoughts you're supposed to put on paper? Make it make sense!

Speech is the source material for writing. Our best writing sounds like us! Have you ever read a text message and recognized who wrote it just by the vocabulary, punctuation style, and emoji selection? Our writing signifies the indelible marks of our personalities and speaking patterns. This is what's known as the writer's "voice." It's that distinct quality of who you are that comes through in your use of language. Writing is merely learning to transcribe that language while applying the appropriate structure. In other words, speaking and writing draw on the same source inside a person.

Of the three skills, then, the first two writing skills (reading and transcription) are more like learning another language. These require explicit instruction (though occasionally some kids who are called "hyperlexic" do learn to read and spell simply through immersion). Learning to decode the alphabet in a variety of fonts, understanding the meaning of the dots, curves, and lines of punctuation—these are the foreign parts of writing for kids.

Self-expression and composition, on the other hand, are natural to children. Nineteenth-century British educator Charlotte Mason puts it beautifully: "'Composition' comes by Nature. In fact, lessons on *composition* should follow the model of that famous essay on 'Snakes in Ireland'—'There are none' . . . If we would believe it, composition is as natural as jumping and running to children who have been allowed due use of books. They should narrate in the first place, and they will compose, later, readily enough; but they should not be taught 'composition.'"

Why would Mason warn against teaching composition to children? Because the moment we impose a structure on these young writers, we make them doubt their natural storytelling abilities—the fluency of their speech. Instead, she recommends using a similar approach to how our children learned to speak. Immerse them in the world of books, urge them to express themselves orally (naturally), and then give them the opportunity to compose their thoughts in writing. Most kids can give an account of what's on their mind that makes sense—that is, in fact, composed.

As a child gains fluency in writing, especially in the mechanics, they can then be guided to try a variety of writing genres. Composition formats are writing styles that make use of higher-order organization and thinking. As writers mature, they learn how to modify their speech for the sake of these written formats. It helps to talk about those composition styles the same way we talk about how to adapt our speaking voices to various activities or environments, such as acting, speeches, oral reports, interviews, casual conversations, business presentations, lectures, and formal events. We're still the same person throughout, but we modify how we present a message to suit the particular demands of the oral format and audience. Writing formats are very much the same.

If we start with the notion that the person who speaks is the same person who writes, we reduce the stress of writing by 973 percent (that's an accurate statistic that I just made up). This understanding seems obvious, yet ask yourself this: When you go to write, do you feel comfortable putting whatever comes to mind onto the page or screen? When the audience is unsafe (someone who will judge your writing), do you go through an awkward translation phase: "Hmm, how shall I say this"? Frequently, students convert their thoughts into what they see as careful written language. They "dumb down" the content to suit their not-yet-fluent spelling and punctuation skills. Or they adopt a mock-sophistication to try to sound like their teachers. Or they hide their true perspective to avoid criticism.

The best writing reflects the voice of the writer, as that writer is today. The more we liberate our kids to write like they speak, the more they will grow as writers who can modify their style of speech to suit the task. In short, the writing life starts long before a child can read, because it begins with speech. Let me put it boldly: in many ways, your children can learn to write even before they learn to read! In fact, your home is the best place for your kids to develop as writers. Everything they learn with you will help them succeed in school. As the primary caregiver, you get to guide your children into a life where writing is valued (not graded) and is a source of personal joy and pride. Once your kids catch on to the power of writing for themselves, their school writing will blossom too!

THE SCRAPBOOK METHOD

Before you can convince your children that they have important stuff to say in their writing, you might need to convince *yourself* that they have important stuff to say that is worth putting in writing. In other words, let's start with you! I had five kids endlessly saying the darndest things. Sometimes they made me laugh so hard I'd have to pull the car over. Other times I was so touched by an insight or kind remark, I would tear up.

I realized at one point that I didn't want to forget these tender expressions of early vocabulary, so I started writing them down. I didn't always carry a notebook with me, so I used to scribble their little phrases and comments onto sticky notes or scratch paper or a random three-by-five note card. I jotted down the date and child's name too. Then I tucked these precious quotes into a notebook with pockets. I've still got it!

You can try it too. This week, collect a variety of words, phrases, and statements you overhear from any of your children. Whatever strikes your fancy qualifies. Jot them down!

* Malaprops: "Mazazine" for *magazine*, "Magah" for *grandma*

* Humor: One seventeen-month-old pointing to another seventeen-month-old and saying, "This one talks!"

* Kindhearted comments: "I can do love to you while you cry, Mama."

* New vocabulary: "I want my doll to have a *cornucopia* of new dresses!"

* Surprising facts: "Did you know that the dung beetle is the world's strongest insect and can lift 1,141 times its body weight?"

* Critical thinking: "I wonder why so many religions tell people to be kind to each other."

Get in the habit of paying attention to what your kids say. Notice and jot down their remarks. Read them back another day, letting them know why you thought those words or remarks were worth capturing and saving in writing. As you learn to notice and value your children's speech, you teach them that the content of their minds deserves to be written and read. In fact, you teach that same lesson to yourself as well. A handy lesson for all parties.

Once you have a sense that your children have thoughts worthy of the page or computer screen, how can you persuade your children to write those thoughts for themselves? What stands in the way? In the next chapter, we'll take a look at how typical writing instruction inhibits kids from taking writing risks.

YOUR WRITING ASSIGNMENT

If you have a baby book for any of your kids (don't worry, I know you don't have one for the youngest child), open it. Find the first words your child said that you wrote down. Jot them in your writing notebook, along with any memories that go with that exciting moment. Extra credit: Record a child's misspelling that you consider "adorable" (you might need to squint to see it that way), date it, and celebrate the attempt to spell!

||||||||||||||||||||

CHAPTER 2

Power or Accuracy?

My friend Glenda came to me with a three-ring notebook, in tears. Her kids *h-a-t-e-d* writing. They refused to do it! "What am I doing wrong?" she asked, and then opened a massive, ugly, dark blue writing manual to the first assignment. It's amazing how much I didn't even like the *look* of it.

Taking the manual from her, I read a sample descriptive paragraph, followed by instructions for the teacher to read to a child. I blinked. "Glenda, did you *read* this sample paragraph?"

"Uh, yeah, I did."

"Did you like it?"

"What do you mean?"

"When you read the sample paragraph, did you think to yourself: *Wow! That's so good, I wish there were a second paragraph!*"

She got flustered. "Um, no? I can't remember what it says."

I gently closed the notebook. "If the sample paragraph is

this forgettable, why would you want your children to learn to write by following this model?"

Glenda didn't know.

THAT DASTARDLY TOPIC SENTENCE

It's funny. When I read the writing I like best, I can't always find the "topic sentence." Sometimes it's buried in the middle of the paragraph. Sometimes it's the "gotcha" line at the end. In this paragraph you're reading right now, the first sentence says that something is funny. But to find out what I consider giggle-worthy, you have to keep reading. The first sentence is not a complete road map to the content of the paragraph as we are often taught is required. Over time, my brain has naturally learned how to lure a conversation partner into a dialogue through bursts of communication. In writing, the mystery of my short two-word sentence "It's funny" does that for a reader. You automatically think, "What's funny?" and keep reading.

If a third-grade teacher made me revise the topic sentence of my paragraph about topic sentences, I'd probably have to write, "The topic sentence is often not found at the beginning of a paragraph"—delivering the punch line before you even had a chance to experience the setup. A flat-footed, comprehensive statement like that can drain the life right out of the writing. Professional writers know this. Compare the pretend revision to the two sentences at the beginning of the paragraph before this one, though. What do you notice? The longer, clearer sentence feels bulky and overdressed, while breaking the ideas into two sentences feels lighter, breezier—like a beach cover-up hinting at what's underneath.

Liveliness and power in writing are easy to sacrifice on the altar of correct format. Young writers are guided to do it all the time—and then we wonder why their writing is dull! Answer: Writing that is dull but accurately formatted, punctuated, and spelled has been rewarded with the letter grade A for decades. Meanwhile, kids who fling their messy originality at the page have often been penalized for not following instructions. I keep wondering: *Shouldn't the instructions be to compel the reader to want to keep reading?* That would be an amazing writing rubric!

WHAT COMES FIRST: FORMATS OR STYLE?

One school of thought says that kids ought to learn writing formats first and then add their unique writing voice and style later. The belief is that a child is freed to write well if they know the structure first. The other school of thought asserts that unruly free expression preserves the writing voice so that when the student learns the formats, writing with personal style within a given format comes naturally. Cards on the table: I'm the second kind of chap.

After working with more than 250,000 families in our Brave Writer program, it's become abundantly clear to me that kids who feel good about what they express in writing are far more motivated to learn the forms. Makes sense, right? The child who's taught formats first, however, may find it difficult to inject their liveliness later, because to their minds, that liveliness interferes with the very formats they were taught! Many adults edit that liveliness right out of a child's writing (and their own).

I remember doing this to one of my early students, a thirteen-year-old athlete I'll call Leah. Leah wrote a fabulous freewrite about running. It was lively in all the right ways—metaphors, similes, vivid verbs. It also included almost no punctuation or capital letters. She wrote it in a big hurry. When I read it aloud to audiences at conferences, I have to suck in a huge draft of air to get through it if I obey the punctuation (or lack thereof!). See how it feels to read Leah's freewrite at the pace the punctuation requires:

> running is so fast just the world feels like it will start running to pass someone up gives you encouragement when you run it feels like running from a predator especially when you run a race the wind howls in your ears even though there isn't any I feel like running even when I'm tired seeing people run reading their minds they have determination DO NOT fail! I don't know why but your feet just go when you stretch it's as boring as an ice cream lid but you know it's for the good working out it's so hard your muscles are like liquid when you are hurting you walk like a flamingo and a wobbling animal mix yet when you run you feel revived you have a pet skunk named goober you have to run from everything bad just imagine everything you hate behind you then just run away from it fast like anything I can't write it's silly my dog runs faster without even really trying then my hand hurts so when you run you can't feel like anything is holding you back

Are you gasping for air? Do you feel like you ran a mile? Perfect! I love how Leah even included that her hand hurt and she "can't write." I'm a runner, and that's exactly how running feels to me—I'm looking at the horizon, willing myself forward, and have the sudden thoughts "My feet hurt" and "I can't run." She's got these glorious similes ("muscles are like liquid," "a flamingo and a wobbling animal mix") and hilarious and precise images ("pet skunk named goober," "everything you hate behind you"). The entire freewrite is filled with insight too ("the wind howls in your ears even though there isn't any," "it's silly my dog runs faster without even really trying"). By the end of this burst of breathless writing, it's clear Leah *knows* running. She isn't trying to follow a format as much as she's exploring the lived experience of moving her body at a tiring pace!

During revision, I made an error as a novice writing coach. I guided Leah to add the missing punctuation and capital letters to her freewrite. She did as directed. When we read her description in its "corrected" form, we were both shocked to discover that we had crushed the life out of the piece. It felt stilted and awkward. What happened? The original draft is literally a *run-on sentence* for a piece about *running*! Without punctuation, the reader is exhausted and out of breath by the end—exactly how you feel when you run! In other words, we had edited the *power* out of the writing in favor of mechanical *correctness*. Together we decided: let's put the freewrite back into its original form and enjoy the raw burst of self-expression that captured what it is to run.

Understanding the goal of writing to be power rather than accurately copyedited text is the beginning of a huge breakthrough in how you guide your young writers. Once a child experiences connecting with a reader in that initial burst of writing, the task of punctuating the piece becomes more meaningful. As an author, your child will be able to consider punctuation choices that suit the content. That process will come later and will be guided by the goals of the writing. In most cases, this means applying the standard conventions of written English, but there are always exceptions—like Leah's freewrite. The key idea to take away here is that punctuation *serves the content*, not the other way around!

THE ART OF IMITATION

In an attempt to be helpful to children, some writing programs suggest that the first step toward original writing is to imitate adult writers. The belief is that a child will be guided to produce more powerful writing if they adopt the voices of successful writers whose words have endured for hundreds or even thousands of years. Pretty high bar for a second grader!

The problem with that philosophy is adults write differently than kids under age eighteen. When imitating an adult writer, the child is being taught subliminally that they need to adopt an inauthentic style of self-expression in order to be successful. As a result, children frequently feel like nothing of who they are is present in their school writing. This experience becomes demotivating. Assigned writing feels more like a chore or a performance rather than self-expression. Meanwhile, the quirky, adorable, clever human you love is edited right out of their work!

Each year, the writer your child was the year before is gone, and a new writer emerges. If we think about photographs of our children, we would never want to doctor their childhood pictures to make them look like the adults they will eventually become. Likewise, in writing, our goal is to capture that gorgeous mind life at each age and stage of growth, from eight to eleven to fifteen and beyond! Your kids will create a written record of who they are, every bit as precious as the annual school portrait.

Let's cut to the chase. It takes trust and a willingness to "play hooky"—to ditch the format-driven teaching you think will save your young writers. I'm here to recommend that you take that risk. Try this pathway first—the one that supports the natural stages of growth that young people go through to become fluent writers. The more advanced academic formats can be adopted once a child feels the power of their writing voice. And, hey, if the experiment fails, the tedious format-first writing program your kids hate will be there waiting for you to adopt it.

OF CLASSROOMS AND FROGS

Picture this. You're charged with designing a curriculum to teach children to write. You don't consider yourself a professional writer. You're an educator. You know how to design lesson plans and inspire students from the front of the classroom. Your job is to create writing lessons that lead to mastery of specific mandated skills, such as proper spelling, correct punctuation, and several age-appropriate formats as outlined in the common core. These skills need a metric—a way to evaluate whether or not your students are progressing toward the established standards.

You decide that you want to teach third graders how to write a descriptive paragraph. How might you design that program? First, you look for a high-quality written description of an item. You analyze why it works—what about that description makes it readable and interesting? Next, you create a rubric for what ought to be in a descriptive paragraph based on this model, and you put those elements in a list to guide your student writers. Then you craft a simple sample paragraph that matches the objectives you want your students to achieve, which you read aloud to them. Next, you explain how to write a similar paragraph, reading the instructions:

* Write a five- to six-sentence descriptive paragraph of any item.

* Begin with a topic sentence.

* Include three to four supporting sentences that appeal to the five senses.

* Close with a sentence that sums up the point of the paragraph.

* Remember to indent the first line.

You provide a single, lined sheet of paper where the students are expected to write the paragraph. They get to pick the item they will describe, but since they're in a classroom, they won't have the item in hand. They'll have to remember what the item is like, think of features to include in the description, put the sentences in order, spell each word correctly, add punctuation, and follow the format.

If your student chose to write about spaghetti, you might get a paragraph like this:

I like spaghetti. The noodles are yellow and curly. The sauce is red. It smells like pizza. It tastes yummy. That's why I love spaghetti.

In some classes, a child who spells and punctuates this paragraph correctly will get an A. This student followed the rubric. It's just that the rubric doesn't include any hint of how to find the words that would make this paragraph more personal and interesting. Instead, the child is supposed to hunt and peck in the air for words the teacher will accept. The complex sentences that would come naturally in a conversation dry up as the student goes to handwrite. Our young writer avoids using terms that they don't know how to spell and sticks with simple sentences that are easy to punctuate. School writing mission accomplished.

Let's shift gears for a moment and investigate your response to this assignment. Did you like reading the student's paragraph? Does it reveal anything about the spaghetti-liker? Could you guess out of a room of kids' paragraphs that this was *your* child's writing? Does it give you a new way to think about spaghetti? Anything else to consider or add to your own experience?

The cool thing about writing as a subject is that students aren't the only ones who are doing it. Countless adults write for a living, and they aren't "graded" by a rubric. Their writing succeeds or fails by their ability to make readers *want to keep reading*. In professional writing courses, the instructor starts with a question: "What do *you* have to say? Why should I bother to read *your* description of spaghetti? What sets *your* insights apart from all the other spaghetti descriptions I might read?" These courses teach adults how to tap into their unique perspective, and then how to improve their vocabulary, insights, and sentence variety to make the writing compelling to read.

These tactics are liberating for writers of all ages and skill levels. Because kids are young and newer to writing, they need a little help understanding the process their minds will go through to write that description. For instance, how can you help a child tap into their memories and insights about spaghetti as they write? What can they do to jostle the word bank inside to see what's there?

To help my child writer, I would begin by boiling water, tossing in noodles, and heating up marinara. My frame of mind: *Let's get up close to spaghetti!* Next, we'd put the prepared spaghetti on a plate so that the writer could taste it and observe it directly while posing relevant experience-based questions to themselves.

* What aroma is this?

* Does the scent remind me of a holiday or time of year?

* What temperature is the sauce on my tongue? Too hot?

* What colors do I see?

* How do the noodles feel as they slither into my mouth? Slippery? Sticky?

* Does the sauce drip down my chin?

* What sound do the noodles make when I slurp them?

* When do I usually eat spaghetti? When did I last eat spaghetti?

* What pattern do the noodles make on the plate?

* Who eats spaghetti with me?

The sensory information is observed in real time and recorded, not just conjured from vague memory. Since there's no structure to apply to the description yet, the writer is free to follow any tangent—to go where the spaghetti takes them, using whatever vocabulary comes. Higher-quality questions lead to better insights and more precise language. As a parent, it's easy to support this kind of writing. You simply offer questions to your child to help them dig a bit deeper, one observation at a time.

Your young writer is encouraged to jot it all down (or you can take notes for them)—the sentence fragments, the observations, the detail, the memories, the quirky terms, the metaphors and anecdotes, the sensations, the seemingly irrelevant ideas, the hard-to-spell words. When it's time to write the paragraph, it's like working with a collection of Tinkertoys or LEGO bricks—looking for the best pieces to build this little house of description. Imagine this possible result:

My brother puts one end of the slippery noodle in his mouth and I put the other end in mine, like Lady and the Tramp. It's a race to the middle, with lots of loud slurping. Right as our two mouths come close together, one of us bites. Usually me, because I chicken out. The noodle snaps. The red sauce splashes a little on my chin. I can taste the bland pasta and the spicy marinara. The aroma reminds me of pizza. The yellow noodles make curlicues on my plate. I hear my parents laughing. I love spaghetti.

This paragraph describes the lived experience of spaghetti. It tells a little story. What we might call the "topic sentence" is at the end; we don't ruin the punch line by putting it at the top. The paragraph starts with a hook that makes the reader wonder, *Why are siblings eating the same noodle?* Yes, there's a sentence fragment in this paragraph. Fragments can be lively! This is a lively paragraph. It includes the descriptive detail the assignment requires. The paragraph is built from reality—a reality the child knows well. As a result, the description is unique to the writer. If this were your child, you could easily pick their spaghetti paragraph out of a lineup of third graders' paragraphs.

Education models of writing instruction tend to see writing the way a biology teacher examines a frog—as something to dissect and understand in a classroom. Professional writers, on the other hand, see writing the way a child sees a frog—as something fascinating and jumpy to play with! It's this distinction that will carry us through the entire book.

BAD WRITERS

The reason so many parents and teachers wilt in the face of unbridled self-expression in writing is that our kids are notoriously "bad writers." Yes, I said it. You look at your child's writing and you don't see brilliance. You see a mess: sloppy handwriting, perplexingly misspelled words, and missing capital letters. Adults expect perfectly copyedited writing in every space they read. In fact, the belief that we are *owed* perfectly copyedited writing underlies the grammar snobbery we see online. Our eyes have been trained to expect a seamless print experience. It's an affront to our delicate natures to tolerate a misplaced apostrophe. Insert shocked emoji!

When our children's "bad writing" badgers our eyeballs, our bodies betray us immediately. We grimace or frown or draw back slightly. We force a fake smile or burst forth with corrections before we've even read the sentence. Our eyes scan for what's missing, rather than noticing what's offered. A child writes, "On cold mornings, I snuggle up with a blanket in my cozy hose." We declare with authority, "You forgot the *u* in *house!*" We don't say, "I'm touched that you feel cozy in our home." Your child paid you a compliment—that matters more than the missing letter *u* on the first read. Correcting the spelling can happen later, after the content has been thoroughly appreciated.

Most traditionally published books go through a series of editorial steps before publication to ensure correct punctuation, spelling, formatting, typesetting, and more. Professional writers know that self-expression in writing does not necessarily mean having perfect skill in copyediting. One author I heard speak said she used to put a sheet of paper filled with commas on top of her typed manuscripts when she sent them to her editor. She attached a sticky note: "Distribute at will." She knew that her job was writing the manuscript. It was her editor's job to fix the rest. My editors in Brave Writer rely on *The Chicago Manual of Style*—more than a thousand pages of the particulars and peculiarities of punctuation, grammar, spelling, and usage—to edit our Brave Writer materials. No one has all of the rules for proper writing mechanics mastered, especially not your nine-year-old.

The professionally published works we enjoy reading are largely error-free, which makes it difficult to face the unwieldy writing of a child in training. But face it we must! We have to fix our attitudes and facial expressions so that our young writers can explore their ideas and stories out from under the harsh glare of our automatic judgment. I recommend practicing in the mirror. Seriously! What does your face look like when you read your child's unedited writing? How can you shift your expression to receive what's offered with gentleness and interest? Can you add a smile or soften your forehead?

The first lesson to hear here is that when we fear our children are bad at writing, it's usually tied up in how their writing *looks* more than how it *reads*. Don't believe me? Next time your child writes, ask them to *read their writing aloud* to you before you have a chance to look at it. One of the quickest ways to get to the heart of their self-expression is to hear the content free from the distraction of messy handwriting and transcription errors. If we see our children's writing as a marvelous jungle rather than a weedy garden, we help our children grow more naturally.

If you've been in the habit of putting accuracy ahead of power in writing, your kids may now be reluctant writers! They don't want to risk getting lambasted again for misspelling the word *because* for the umpteenth time. Instead, focus on the child as a vulnerable little person whose feelings get hurt when you put too much emphasis on the parts of writing that they don't yet know how to do reliably. When I see a student's pain, I get curious rather than insistent. It's important to pay attention to the reactions we create in our young writers, because once the habit of fear is formed, it's much harder to overcome. I often tell parents that the best move they can make is to preserve a child's wonder and interest in writing. If you protect that feeling, your kids will go far.

Truth is, there's a *lot* of pain in the story of writing instruction. When we prioritize writing mechanics—handwriting, spelling, punctuation, grammar, and formats—as the gateway to the right to write, we overlook the risky, interesting self-expression of the writer. We put *accuracy* (of mechanics) over *power* (of writing voice). I often joke that no one ever finished a novel and gave this compliment: "Every comma was perfectly placed. You should read this book!" The commas support the story, not the other way around.

Our kids deserve to know that it's what lives in their minds and hearts that makes their writing sing. There are ways to build skill in the mechanics so that the internet trolls don't abuse your young ambitious writers when they post. Brave Writer has programs available for all ages that train kids in the mechanics of writing without undermining their confidence in their original writing. Today's spell check and grammar check apps offer feedback in an emotionally safe, depersonalized way, with a relatively high degree of accuracy. What computers can't do is provide the content that is uniquely your child's! We teach our kids to handwrite, type, spell, and punctuate well enough so that they can transcribe their own amazing, insightful, hilarious, dark, and deeply meaningful stories, experiences, and ideas. In the next chapter, we'll dive into that beautiful and mysterious world that is the inner lives of your children and teens.

You'll be positively amazed and tickled at what good writers your kids already are, even if they can't spell *hippopotamus* yet.

YOUR WRITING ASSIGNMENT

Write briefly about the emotions you experience when you see a child's "bad writing." How do you react to a child's misspelled word in a Mother's Day card or on a thank-you note to your sister? What happens in your body when your child's handwriting seems illegible or sloppy? How does your face change when you give an assignment and the child writes something completely different from what you were expecting? What would you prefer your reaction to be?

||||||||||||||||||

CHAPTER 3

Your Kids Are Already Writers

D id you know that the writing life starts before your child can read? From the moment we cuddle our toddlers and read *Snuggle Puppy* to them for the first time (of hundreds), we say to our children that writing matters. Each time we read together, we demonstrate that language can live on through a written record. Your child becomes accustomed to hearing the same words preserved and protected in print on every reread too. This practice of valuing words in print leaves an impression on young minds. *These words matter. We read them again and again. They are in books that I can hold in my hands.* Books make language manifest, permanent.

Your kids come to value writing when they value reading. The two ideas hold hands. In fact, it's incredible to realize that most children hold a wildly positive view of writing before they enter school. They're enchanted by the magic of written language—the way words on a page stay put and can be reread every time the parent and child hold the same slim volume in their hands. Reading is simply noting the writing on a page or screen. That's it. Reading and writing: two sides of the same coin (or in this case, book).

Young children participate in the act of writing before they can read too. They make marks on surfaces using a variety of implements. Your pre-readers might scribble what looks like scrawl or versions of the alphabet on a chalkboard, in a notebook, or on scratch paper (or in permanent markers streaked across the kitchen wall). They might draw pictures or attempt to trace an image.

My youngest daughter used to fill composition books with the letters of the alphabet in a random order, both lower- and uppercase, telling us that no one was allowed to read her writing—it was private. She hooked up her mind with her hand, and while she didn't transcribe her thoughts into words we could decode, she very much was "writing." She had understood the assignment: *If I want to preserve my thoughts, I had better write them down.* In this way, she learned to write before she learned to read. When you read to a child, it counts as part of your writing program. Each picture book, each poem, each novel develops your child's writing "ear."

BREAKING THE FOURTH WALL

When my twenty-month-old grandson declared, "Yesssss!!!!" to a question posed by his mom, we all cracked up. He was new to speech, yet he used the perfect intonation and emphasis to convey the sentiment "Yes, duh, obviously!" My daughter Johannah, his aunt, declared: "I love when toddlers are learning to talk. It's like they're breaking the fourth wall." To "break the fourth wall" in acting means to address the audience directly. When a toddler first speaks, it's like all that inner monologue is suddenly directed at an audience: us. What a great metaphor for learning to speak! We talk so that the thoughts that live in our minds can be externalized and delivered to an interested audience. The first words a child says are so riveting to that audience, they're often recorded with real joy in a baby book, on social media, or in a text to a grandparent.

Our talkative toddlers become verbal virtuosos by the time they're around five years old. They spin tales before they can read. The only way their ideas and stories can be preserved, however, is if some kind caregiver takes the trouble to jot down those words on the child's behalf. For the not-yet-reading-or-writing child, this act is akin to participating in magic—words that once vanished into thin air are now made tangible, ready for any reader to enjoy hours or days later!

Unfortunately, many children don't get to have that experience. Maybe you recall entering kindergarten eager to write a story or share your ideas, only to lose heart. Why? Because most writing instruction starts with the premise that the acts of spelling and punctuation are more important than the content of the child's thoughts. What would happen if we treated a child's oral language as worthy of the page *before* that child could handwrite their own thoughts?

When I was raising my kids, I decided to find out. In my house, if a child erupted into a bit of narrative or had something to say that seemed amusing or insightful or valuable to me in any way, I reached for the nearest supermarket receipt or old bank envelope and began jotting down the words as quickly as that child could say them. As I had more children, it became easier to leave clipboards with scratch paper around the house for those out-of-the-blue narratives.

One time, my four-year-old son Liam had amassed a large cluster of LEGO men who each possessed superpowers and creative names. I grabbed a clipboard and asked him to name and describe each one of his little men. To the utter delight of both of us, he went into elaborate detail, and I wrote down every word. Liam carried that clipboard around for a month, standing the little men on each of their descriptions. It struck me that he had paid such good attention, he knew which order I had written them in and was able to associate each LEGO man with the correct name and description, even though he couldn't yet read fluently! The fact that I'd valued his language enough to put it in writing on a clipboard helped build the foundation of his belief that his writing mattered.

I've seen this powerful practice transform countless children's writing lives—including resistant, damaged teen writers. There's something about realizing that what you have to say matters, even before you're able to type or write it yourself, that puts writing into the right perspective—your thoughts *already matter enough to be written.* That's a powerful, life-changing message for anyone, but particularly children.

Jotting down a child's spoken words isn't a shortcut to writing; it is the art of writing itself. Like a secretary taking dictation for a busy executive, adults serve as the speech-to-text conduit for our budding writers. This phase marks the origin of a child's writing journey, where their natural self-expression flows without inhibition, unburdened by spelling or handwriting constraints. They will take up the pencil on behalf of their own thoughts in the next stage of growth. In the meantime, we can wield the pen for them!

CATCH YOUR CHILD IN THE ACT
OF SELF-EXPRESSION

Parents have a bad habit. They believe if they just *tell* their kids what to do and how to do it, they've fulfilled their role as guides and leaders in their children's lives. So much telling. Think about the countless instructions you issue in a day: "Stop jumping on the couch" and "Go put on your shoes" and "Sit still while you finish your math homework." The telling method of parenting feels quick, because you can do it with little thought. And for many commands, kids hop to it and get with the program. With writing, however, this method falls short. It doesn't work to shout, "Just write three sentences!" That command makes kids freeze. I call this the "blank page, blank stare" syndrome: hand your child a blank page, get back a blank stare.

There's a reason for that frozen stare—a child's brain shakes the words clear like an Etch A Sketch the moment they're asked to write. The pressure to coordinate handwriting, spelling, punctuation, *and* their own thoughts becomes a traffic jam in their mind. Even if they have a wonderfully sophisticated vocabulary when speaking, suddenly they have to pause to consider which letters go first and what punctuation marks follow. Once a child puts their mind into editing mode, the great complex ideas evaporate from their imagination. Suddenly, all that's left is an empty space where the thought used to be. That's why they wilt and shrug their shoulders and tell you they can't think of anything to write. They aren't lying! They really can't. The words went on walkabout, and they're left standing in a language desert.

Let's back up. What would happen if *you* took the role of secretary at that moment? How might your child's active, lively mind find its way to the page if *you* relieved your child of the pressure to transcribe those thoughts? You can find out, today! Ready?

Jot down your child's words the next time they *spontaneously* erupt in speech.

Picture this scenario. You're in the kitchen, stir-frying dinner. Your eight-year-old son, Herbert, bounds in from the backyard, where he was playing with his dog, Holly. Herbie breathlessly launches into a tale about how Holly saw a squirrel and chased it across the yard to a tree. The moment you notice that Herbie is in the white-hot heat of self-expression, you turn off the stove. You grab the nearest bank statement envelope, flip it over, and start writing down Herbie's *exact words*.

Your son may be startled by this behavior. He may ask, "Mom, what are you doing?"

Simply reply: "This is so good, I don't want to forget it, so I'm writing it down."

Return to scribbling his little tale as quickly and accurately as you can. Some kids immediately square their shoulders and go on for several more minutes. They feel proud of what they have to express and want you to record *all* of it. Some kids may feel nervous and ask you to stop writing so that you look them in the eye. If you have this kind of child, simply set down the pencil, listen intently, and as soon as your child finishes sharing, jot down as much of their little narrative as you can remember, in words as close to your child's as possible.

That evening, when the family is gathered at dinner, whip out the envelope and announce, "I was chatting with Herbie today, and he told me the story of how Holly chased a squirrel in the backyard. It was so good I wrote it down. I want to read it to you now." Then read, with pleasure and approval. When you get to the end of the little tale, ask follow-up questions: "And then what happened? Did the squirrel get away?" Value the writing as communication. In fact, there's no need to explicitly call it writing. It's clear that that is what it is!

After dinner, take that envelope with the words you jotted down and toss it into the library basket with all the books you've checked out. For the next few weeks, when you read aloud to your kids, particularly to sweet little Herbie, pull out the envelope and say, "Oh look! Here's the story about Holly by Herbert. Let's read this one again." Give your child the joy of *being seen as an author*, in the same category as the authors of the books you schlep home from the library.

This act of writing down what your kids say spontaneously is like a secret handshake. You're admitting your child into the club of writers. You're giving your child a direct experience of what writing is—the transcription of valuable thoughts to be read by others. By putting your child's words in writing for them, you demonstrate what you now believe: that a writer lives inside your child's body and is merely in search of a transcriptionist. Pre-readers, kids with language delays, intimidated writers, and bored teens need to experience that their thoughts are valuable. The words that are natural to them are already important enough to be written and read—it is *these* words that should show up on the page when *they* write.

Any of your children's freely offered thoughts can be recorded—whether it's a recitation of all facts pertaining to the black-capped chickadee, an enumeration of the dimensions of the tallest roller coaster in the country, or a retelling of your child's favorite Disney movie. Jotting down their thoughts does two things well. First, it demonstrates your faith in your child as a writer already. Second, it lets your child practice their narrative skills by attempting to compose ideas and stories into a coherent retelling. As you write down your child's thoughts, they may backtrack or start over or skip ahead to what is most interesting. Because they're speaking, they have that flexibility. Simply take what they offer and get it down. You don't need to help them organize or restate. Let them find their own sequence of thoughts.

The jot-it-down method can be used for all ages, but I especially recommend it for your kids who are pre-readers. When you show them that their words and experiences are worthy of being written now before they can do it for themselves, they become more eager to learn to write when the time comes. Even older kids who struggle to see the value in writing deserve to experience their ideas being transcribed and read back to them. Jotting down a child's freely offered ideas is the starting point for reclaiming writing for a resistant writer of any age.

JOTTING IT DOWN WITH TEENS

You can try the jot-it-down strategy with your teens too. I recommend waiting until you're in a debate about some issue that matters to your teen. In the heat of the conversation, stop talking and grab a sheet of scratch paper. Write down the teen's reasoning—why they believe the way they do. Capture their ideas word for word, and at dinner, pull out the sheet of paper. Say: "Sophie was telling me why she thinks she should be allowed to drive downtown alone to attend acting lessons. I haven't been on board, but she made some good arguments, so I wrote them down. I want to read them so we can discuss this situation." Then read what you jotted down and discuss.

When we write down what someone else expresses, they feel valued. Heck, I've even heard that this act of jotting down what someone says is effective in marriages. When you give the other person's thoughts so much weight that you're willing to put their words in your own handwriting, the other person has a direct experience of being heard. That act can go a long way in de-escalating conflict too. The point here is that writing makes thought permanent. Permanence implies value. Value leads to risk-taking. Risk-taking builds skills. The old method of performing skills before they're consolidated is failing so many children. Why not try this other method and see what happens in your family?

Sometimes parents tell me that they have tried this idea and it bombed. They say to a child, "Tell me a story, I'll write it down for you," and the child balks. In truth, asking a child to speak so you can write it down doesn't always work. The moment you *ask* for the words, your child will feel pressured to perform—similar to how they feel when you ask them to write. The key to this practice is catching your child in the act of *spontaneous* self-expression. Once they start speaking freely, notice that, and without a word, jot down their exact sentences.

If this practice catches on, you may discover that later, once you've built trust, you can ask for a narrative or a story or an explanation of steps. In our family, I had kids bringing me paper and pens so that I would write down their thoughts for them. Over time, they got tired of waiting for me to write and took up the pencil themselves. We'll talk about how to make that transition in the coming chapters. Not to worry—you won't have to keep jotting down your child's thoughts until they go to college!

That said, sometimes it's hard to trust a process like this. What I've noticed is that when adults lack confidence in their own writing abilities, they transfer that anxiety to their kids unwittingly. In order to create conditions for freedom and risk-taking in writing, it helps to start by healing the damaged writer that lives in you. We're going to do just that in the next chapter.

YOUR WRITING ASSIGNMENT

‖‖

Try the jot-it-down activity. Then open up your writing notebook and write about how it went!

CHAPTER 4

IIIIIIIIIIIIIIIIIIIII

Healing the Damaged Writer in You

I've never seen a writing manual address this particular elephant in the room: many adults are themselves damaged writers. The adults who enjoy writing usually come to it through at least one of three ways: they discovered writing for pleasure outside of school, they read early and had a knack for the mechanics that earned them teachers' approval, or they were raised by parents who delighted in their writing. If you did not luck into this trifecta of writing bliss, you may be one of the ones who still feels a twinge of anxiety when you send an email or are called on to write for publication or graduate school.

Naturally, there are some remarkable teachers in school environments who give kids the confidence they need to grow as writers. My mother, a professional author, remembers her third-grade teacher, who helped her students turn their writing into little books that she then housed on a bookshelf in class. Students could read each other's stories by checking out the student-books using a method similar to library loans. My mother recalls how enthralled she was. Her teacher made a beautiful suggestion: "Maybe one day your books will be in libraries outside of school." My mom thought to herself, "Yes, that's what I'm going to do!" Seventy-two books later, I'd say she reached her goal. Can you see how powerful it is to show a child's writing has value, to find earnest readers for it, and to suggest that each of us has the capacity to find readers who care for the writing we do?

Unfortunately, a performance-based approach to writing often conditions us to believe that grades and critiques are the best approach to writing growth. After all, those scores, check marks, and grades must mean something! If we simply *enjoy* a child's writing for what it is, will that child improve? How can we be sure? And so, the same adults who suffered humiliation under a system of scrutiny often double down on those same methods for their own children. There's something about having struggled that makes a person believe that struggle is the right way to learn. We associate struggle with diligence or effort rather than seeing it as it ought to be seen—a sign of pain and distress. Diligence and effort can be pleasurable or satisfying. They don't have to be painful (nor should they be) to prove their merit. The way we teach writing ought to create an environment where a child *wants* to be diligent, where a child *cares* to put in effort.

One mother who took one of our Brave Writer writing classes shared a perfect example of this experience. Her twelve-year-old son had received a video game for his birthday right during the six-week class. At the time, he was immersed in writing a story whose ending did not yet satisfy him. He asked his mother if he could rewrite the ending. When she said yes, he went on to not only rewrite the ending but to expand his draft into four chapters. He told his brothers to go ahead and play his new game while he recopied and edited the final draft. When a child is captivated by the power of their own writing, it can be more compelling than a video game!

Parents are notorious for getting more rigid and serious when they feel anxious about their children's skill development. If you doubt your own capacity as an adult who writes, you're likely to be harder on your child as a fledgling writer. You'll worry that the mistakes they make are permanent or mean more than they really do. That fear will cause you to be uptight and to expect flawless writing rather than risky writing.

My son-in-law George is a professional muralist. He paints huge canvases, using his home as his art studio. My daughter, who's not an artist, worried that their toddler would ruin the paintings if he were in the same room with his dad while he painted. Interestingly, George had no such qualms about protecting his artwork. His confidence in painting freed him to let his son playfully participate. He handed a paintbrush to his toddler son, who boldly made big splashes of paint on the canvas alongside his father's. Naturally, George painted over those bold brush marks once his son left the room. But what did my grandson learn? That paint is for painting! That paintbrushes are for making bold strokes! He is learning at a young age that he is worthy of paint and canvas and that he doesn't have to worry about "getting it right" in order to participate.

To create the right atmosphere for writing growth, we want to give maximum space for lots of careless words. Unfortunately, if you don't feel comfortable with writing yourself, you may not know how to give that space. That's why it's important to heal the damaged writer that lives in you as you teach your child. So let's do that now!

WHEN WRITING INSTRUCTION CAUSES HARM

The other night, in a professional setting, I met a man in his sixties—let's call him Ken—who has built multiple seven- and eight-figure companies from scratch. He asked about my work. When I told him my company teaches kids how to write in ways that reduce the drama and trauma of writing, his face fell. "I wish I had had that as a child," he said. I told him that many adults heal their writing distress when they enroll in our writing classes with their children. He was surprised by this strategy—enrolling parents and children together? I explained that in our program, we treat the parent and child as a team and teach them how to be partners and allies in the writing process. He shook his head and launched into the story of a scarring memory.

In fifth grade, Ken wrote a short story that was three pages long. His friends and his mother read it and told him it was a very good story. "I put my whole heart into it, Julie," he told me, his voice cracking with emotion. "I got back two letter grades: A for content and F for grammar. All I could see was the F. I've never put my heart into writing again. If I have to write on a whiteboard in front of my employees, I freeze and panic. I only use voice-to-text software now for writing or texting. I never want to feel that humiliation again."

Imagine being a completely successful adult and still being dominated by a fear of misspelling a word or forgetting a punctuation mark!

I told him, "It didn't have to be that way. I'm sorry that the F stole your joy in the story."

And then he broke and tears came. I watched this sixty-nine-year-old man dissolve into a ten-year-old boy right in front of my eyes.

Another woman—let's call her Sarah—once shared with me that in seventh grade, after her mother had died, she was inspired to write a short story that expressed her heightened emotions. A few weeks later, her English teacher announced to their class that the story had earned the highest score on a standardized test in the entire middle school. Sarah was startled, as she hadn't seen herself as a high achiever. Just as she began to feel the wonder of this accomplishment, the English teacher continued to speak to Sarah in front of the whole class. She cautioned Sarah not to get too excited because the piece wasn't perfect and there was still much work to do. Sarah described the feeling as "crushing." She had written a "part of her soul" in a way that the whole school had recognized as valuable—but that still wasn't enough to avoid public criticism from her teacher. She hasn't written for pleasure since.

Over the years, I've practically become a therapist for parents who have writing wounds from childhood. They want to teach their kids to write, but their own traumatic memories stand in their way. Sometimes they become even more rigid and perfectionistic with their children because they want to protect their kids from online bullies and harsh schoolteachers. Naturally, doubling down on the methods that brought you pain simply creates more pain. But their fears are warranted. People can be cruel over the smallest typos. Here are a few memories parents have shared with me over the years. See if any of them remind you of an experience with writing that stole your confidence:

* "I was told to go into math because I'm a terrible writer."

* "I never earned more than a B on a paper. I got the same teacher comments again and again, but no matter what I tried to do to improve, my grade never budged. I stopped trying so hard and still got Bs. I learned that I'm not good at writing and I don't know how to improve."

* "I was accused of plagiarism on the best paper I ever wrote. I defended myself, but the teacher didn't believe me. The paper was disqualified from my cumulative grade, and I felt nervous to write 'too well' in the future. I stopped trying."

* "I have dyslexia. It went undiagnosed when I was a kid. Every time a teacher identified a misspelling, I felt stupid. I could never get an A, because I couldn't spell."

* "I was too self-conscious to show my writing to other kids in the class. I'm an introvert. I hated 'peer review' and hearing feedback from my friends."

* "I'm writing my PhD dissertation right now. No one has given me any guidance on how to structure it. I'm floundering. I'm embarrassed to ask for help."

* "My teacher used to put samples of our writing on a big screen in class. She would then analyze what was wrong with the paper. Even though she blocked out our names, I always knew which paper was mine. It was humiliating to listen to her tear my writing apart in front of everyone."

WRITING TRAUMA

Why do we do this to students? Writing trauma is real. It's also entirely unnecessary. We humans are so strongly identified with the words we communicate (in writing, in speaking) that critique can feel like an insult to our very souls, especially when we're young. Even as I write these words, I can hear the refrain coming back to me: "But if we don't correct what's wrong, how will the writing improve?" That's the sneaky trick of the whole system, though. No one thrives under a standard of perfection. Room for trial and error, freedom to take risks, and guidance that is understanding and insightful lead to the best outcomes for any new skill a person wants to learn. Let's not treat writing like it's the one subject where we're free to give insulting corrections and expect that those insults won't leave lasting scars.

I'm appalled at the way writing is often taught. Why do we think that it's okay to point out everything wrong with someone's writing? What morality have we adopted that says, "My ability to find fault in your writing is more important than your effort to convey your ideas to me"? Why is writing instruction treated as though it's divorced from our emotional lives? Why do we think it helps the writer in any way to point out all their spelling errors? If a child knows how to spell a word, they'll spell it correctly. If a word is misspelled in a paper, that means the student doesn't know how to spell it yet. Correcting it after the fact is pointless. All that act does is prove that the *teacher* knows how to spell that word. By identifying a misspelling (which is often the only feedback on a paper), you teach the student that their writing isn't worthy of admiration yet—that until they turn in a flawless manuscript, they will never earn the pleasure of having been read.

So what's going wrong? Why is everyone obsessed with the mechanics of writing? Spelling and punctuation are easy to correct because they obey conventions that apply across the board to everyone. The content of a person's thoughts, however, requires a more subjective and rigorous engagement. If you're a teacher with twenty-five to one hundred papers to grade—or a parent who's insecure about their own writing abilities—the quickest remarks you can make focus on copyedits, not substantial engagement with ideas or storyline.

We'll talk about how to grow spelling skills in chapter 11, but honestly, that's so low on the ledger of ideas to discuss when we talk about writing, I put that conversation near the end of this book. You can flip there now if you like, but I warn you: if you think getting your kids to spell well is the key to writing, you'll wind up with stories similar to the ones I mentioned above.

One of the issues kids face in school is that the teacher is the de facto authority in class. Kids see the teacher's critique as "official." Yet when it comes to writing, the one *doing the writing* is actually in the position of authority over their own thoughts and ideas. In fact, the words *author* and *authority* both share the Latin root *auctor*, which means "originator" or "promoter." Over time, they've evolved and acquired distinct meanings and usages. *Author* connotes creative production, while *authority* is associated with expertise and influence. How about we endow our kids with both authority *and* authorial control over their writing? What would happen if we deeply respected both their creative output and their expertise on their own thoughts? What if they had the authority to take or ignore our suggestions? What if we treated their writing as something meaningful to them rather than as a performance for us? This is what we can do for our children!

HEAL THE DAMAGE

We build kids' confidence in their writing by enthusiastically receiving what they offer. A writer grows when given practical instruction to help them achieve their goals—usually by being read and appreciated as a thinker and storyteller. It's really pretty simple. Good writing instruction starts with letting go of our neurotic need to control the picky details of the writing.

So how can you become a confidence-builder rather than an obsessive editor of your child's writing, oh damaged writer who is an adult? Here are a few steps to help you heal first. By the way, if you're a free, unburdened writer, you can skip ahead to the next chapter. Or, if you like, read along and think about your friends who may need your kind intervention to heal from their writing hurts too. The processes and practices I share in this book will create the conditions for writing growth at home. You can best prepare your family if you follow this guidance.

To heal the damaged writer in you, I recommend cultivating a writing life now. It's okay if you don't like writing. The goal here isn't to become a writer or even to love writing. Instead, it's a bit like getting over any fear—do it as a gift to yourself. Take it in teaspoons.

1. **Each time I share a writing practice, try it yourself.**

   If I suggest you jot down your child's words on their behalf, try recording your own unedited thoughts as a voice memo on your phone or with voice-to-text software on your computer. Convert your oral language into writing just as I'm asking you to do for your child. Now read your transcribed words. Notice the difference in how you feel as you self-express without the burden of transcription. Any freer? Do you feel a little guilty, as if it doesn't count? Do you wonder if you're cheating? Ask a spouse or friend to jot down your words as you speak. Notice what that feels like. If you have painful memories, acknowledge them, then let them go. If the feelings persist, ironically, you can journal about them! Or discuss them over brunch with a good friend. You're no longer in school. You're safe. You'll be okay. The ideas come first. Improving mechanics comes second.

2. **Write with your children.**

   As Pat Schneider, one of my favorite writing mentors, reminds us: When teaching anyone to write, everyone should take the same writing risks. If you want your kids to write poems, write a poem too. If you introduce mind-mapping to your children, make a mind-map of your own first. When you teach freewriting, set the timer, sit at the table with your kids, and write! If your child is learning to conduct research for a paper, try your hand at citations, paraphrases, and summaries before you teach these skills to your student. Do the very writing practices you ask of your child. If your child is a school student (as opposed to a homeschool student), try doing some of their homework assignments for yourself. Not only will you build empathy, you'll also gain skill and confidence.

3. **Find a safe corner of the internet where you can write.**

For me, it's a private Gmail account I use as a diary that no one reads but me. For you, it might be a social media account or blog set up under an alias. Keep it unlisted, or only allow safe people to read what you share or post. You can also create a small text messaging group with friends and tackle some topics together—like reviewing books or films, writing about your childhoods, or exploring dreams for the future. Be sure to let everyone know that this is not a space to correct each other's grammar, spelling, or punctuation. Tiptoe back into writing for others so you can feel comfortable and competent.

4. **You're not in a hurry.**

It's okay to take time. The best writing contexts are spacious. The best writing goes through multiple revisions. If you write something and you find it dull or childish (that's how I often feel about my first drafts), set the writing aside for a week. Return to it with fresh eyes and read it again. Say to yourself: "I can make any changes I would like to. The first draft is a map to what I want to say, not necessarily how I want to say it." As you give yourself room to grow in your writing skills, you'll find yourself being far kinder and more supportive to your kids as they grow in theirs too.

5. **Have a snack.**

   Yep, there's research in the field of occupational therapy that recommends a suck-swallow-breathe practice to support concentration. Moving your mouth while you write promotes focus. One of my writing friends chews gum. I sip tea. Sometimes I eat potato chips. Give yourself permission to support the hard work of writing with something tasty for your mouth. (*Psst*—this works amazingly well with kids too!)

OVERCOMING PERFECTIONISM

Your confidence in writing instruction will grow as you gain confidence in the writing process for yourself. Sometimes watching your children become free, at-ease writers is enough to liberate you to be the coach they need. I've found, though, that if you have a terribly perfectionistic approach to writing as a holdover from school, the only way to transcend it is to enter into a writing practice yourself. It is the best step you can take to throw off the shackles of the old "ghost of school past" that haunts you as you try to guide your young writers.

As I like to say, perfectionism is inherited. Children get it from their parents. If your kids are afraid to make mistakes in writing, that's frequently because somewhere along the way they learned that you would be happier with their writing if they didn't. (They may also learn this from school.) The best way to reverse this particular curse is to make writing mistakes yourself in front of your kids in your own handwriting. You can also rehabilitate yourself by giving your children the kindness and support you craved when you were young. I've developed a strategy for how to offer that support, which I'll share with you in chapter 6. Before we do that, you probably wonder how you'll know if your child is producing good writing. Let's get that sorted out first.

YOUR WRITING ASSIGNMENT

Write a bit about the damage that occurred in your childhood around writing. Tell the truth. You can burn the page in the fireplace or permanently delete the file once you finish. Get it all out. If it was particularly traumatic, try writing about it four times for fifteen minutes each. Stay focused on a particular upsetting incident. Complete these four sessions within a week. You may notice a distinct change in how you feel about writing once you give yourself permission to look squarely at the harm caused to you.

‖‖‖‖‖‖‖‖‖‖‖‖‖‖‖‖

CHAPTER 5

Good Writing Is Surprising Writing

You know good writing when you read it. The key evidence? You *keep reading.*

Good writing is determined by the reader. Certainly there are official bodies that seek to award *great* writing (like the Nobel Prize in Literature). But that's not what I mean by *good* writing. If we limit the definition of "good" to writing that wins awards, we overlook the good writing we read every single day for our own education, pleasure, and entertainment. Good writing is *everywhere*—even found in places we might initially consider unlikely, like TikTok captions, romance novels, and comic books. Who determines what constitutes good writing is up for grabs! I submit for your examination the notion that *you*, dear reader, get to decide what you consider to be "good writing."

Now that I've endowed you with those powers, you can confer them on your kids as well. The key question to ask is this: *Why do I like this writing?* When you can identify why a bit of writing makes you laugh or gives you pause or ups your level of interest, you're stumbling into the neighborhood of literary devices that create that good writing you so enjoy! What I've noticed? The kids who understand how to use the tactics that make their writing pop and sparkle feel far freer to take those writing risks than their grade-weary adults. Schools can trick students into thinking good writing is the kind that's well copyedited and gets a good grade from a teacher. But we know from our own reading experience that our favorite writing is the kind that makes us want to *keep reading*.

Sometimes the good writing you like is poorly spelled or mispunctuated. Yet, if the writing is compelling enough, you'll sweep those missteps aside to see where this piece of writing is going. (I see this happen frequently on Reddit discussion boards!) Not all compelling writing is well thought out or logical either. What makes writing "good"—the kind you might pay to read, the kind you might read well past your bedtime, the type of writing that makes your blood boil—is that you feel entertained, provoked, or uniquely informed by it. If you don't care about what you've read after reading it, can we call it good writing? The best writing makes its ideas, instructions, stories, opinions, experiences, and information interesting. That's the job of the writer—to get you to *care*.

One of the ways writers provoke you into caring is by doling out surprises throughout the article, essay, poem, novel, work of nonfiction, or song lyric. Writers use surprise in a whole host of ways. For instance, they might cite a surprising statistic. (Did you know that Marcel Proust's *In Search of Lost Time* is the longest book ever published, coming in at 1.3 million words?) They might quote an industry expert expressing an unexpected opinion. (Toni Morrison famously tells writers to write what they *don't* know—contrarian advice!) Story-tellers are great at surprising their readers with plot twists. (Who saw Frodo refusing to toss the ring into the fiery depths of Mordor once he got there?) Other writers are funny. (*Calvin and Hobbes,* anyone?) Clever metaphors and comparisons are a staple of great writing, forcing the reader to see the familiar in fresh ways. ("Time flies, messy as the mud on your truck tires" from Taylor Swift's "'Tis the Damn Season" shifts how we hear the "time flying" cliché.)

When kids discover that writing can be funny, ironic, silly, or shocking, they're much more interested in doing it! They love to make you laugh or think. They get a kick out of using sophisticated vocabulary or daring you to reject their writing when they include graphic language. One of my students went into gross (I mean it!) detail about their own digestive system—I can't unsee the train of poop moving through the tunnel of the intestine. Kids are gleeful when they can pop off with a list of facts you don't know about their topic of choice. Sometimes kids will spark your interest through an original comparison—like calling their white furry puppy a formidable yeti.

What really burns my biscuits is the fact that traditional writing instruction doesn't even bother to mention the role of surprise in writing. It's the invisible literary element that gets routinely bounced from the club. Yet once your kids catch on to surprise as the key ingredient in good writing, they discover a mission worth adopting. They *want* to catch you off guard with their cleverness!

So let's dive into this splish-splashy pool of linguistic delight together. Now that you know what makes writing good, the next question is: *Whodunit?* Who are these *good* writers who know how to dole out surprises in a steady drip drip drip of stimulating writing? Bestselling novelists? News journalists? Professors on college campuses? Certainly you'll find powerful writing in all these places. But there's one uncelebrated writing hero that I want to feature in this chapter. The humble sports journalist is often overlooked—as though they aren't doing "real" writing or journalism. In my opinion, however, it is the sportswriter who happens to be among the top workhorse writers on the planet. (Bold statement, right? I'm here to *surprise* you with my unique take on this topic! Are you still reading? Good—I hooked you!)

Think about it with me. The sports journalist has a monumental task: to write about a sporting event that has already occurred. They have to whip together an article in the wee hours after a game on a tight deadline. The scores are in, the injured players are soaking in an ice bath, the coaches are drawing up plays for the next game, and sports fans like you and me already know who won and lost. We probably even watched the game! In the old days, before television and the internet, fans relied on the sports page of their local newspaper to describe the game for them in sparkling detail so they could experience a version of it in their imaginations. Today's sportswriter has a much bigger challenge: to write about *a game we've already seen.* The spectacular plays and the controversial calls? Already well known, dissected on social media, replayed on cable TV, and debated on radio. What could a sportswriter possibly say about a game that is over?

This is where a *good* writer shines. The sports journalist helps us relive that valuable event by writing about it in surprising ways. Humans *love* to relive their experiences. Case in point: every pop lyricist makes a living writing about falling in love. In a similar way, the sportswriter is retelling a story fans want to experience again. These journalists are experts at applying the power of surprise to keep us reading something that on the surface doesn't seem surprising at all.

One of my favorite sportswriters is the award-winning journalist Gene Wojciechowski. He's got the trifecta of what good writing should be: insight, vivid language, and surprise. When interviewed about what makes a great sportswriter, he cited a friend's description as the inspiration for his style of writing: "Shelby Strother told me a long time ago there should always be a guy walking through a window into your bedroom that you're not ready for. You have to set the reader up." I find it incredible that when telling the interviewer what makes great writing, Gene uses a powerful, visceral metaphor. The best writing lays a trap so the reader walks right into it and then fights to the end of that piece of writing to untangle the meaning.

One of my favorite Wojciechowski articles described a UCLA basketball beatdown of the LSU Tigers during March Madness in 2006. This was a game where LSU lost 59 to 45—one of the lowest total scores in the tournament that year. What can be said about a game where the outcome is one-sided and the defense won handily with no flashy shots or spectacular offense? I picture Wojciechowski cracking his knuckles and flexing his fingers as he warms them up for his keyboard. He delves into his memory bank of boring experiences and delivers this surefire opening hook: "If you love watching sweat dry, C-SPAN and the 12-disc DVD series on the history of Baroque Period painting, you'll love watching a replay of UCLA squeezing the Final Four life out of LSU." Immediately we get the point—that boring game we watched? Yeah, it was *really* boring.

Wojciechowski's challenge was to keep his readers reading,

which meant his writing had to be more entertaining than the game (ironically!). He captured the effect of that brutal defense in another clever metaphor: "The Bruins don't simply play defense, they roll you in bubble wrap, apply duct tape and send you home in an overnight package." Instantly, your mind pictures an absurd scenario—a collection of oversize college kids, wrapped in plastic, being shipped back to Baton Rouge via UPS.

When we read great writing, we're treated to a cascade of literary devices deployed to surprise us. We should learn how to write a good simile or comparison not just because an English teacher says so but because these devices are the power tools of writing! They deliver a gut punch or tickle your funny bone. They delight, amaze, explain, and reassure. Skilled writers know this. You know who else excels at deploying these kinds of surprising elements? Kids! But in order to use these tools, they need to know what they are. Before they can be clever writers, they can benefit from analyzing the writing they like to read.

DELIGHTFUL DEVICES

A game you can play with your kids is to ask them what makes them want to keep reading—the novel, the social media posts, the text messages from a friend, the nonfiction library book. What is it about this sentence, fact, paragraph, or idea that pushes your child to read more? For instance, can we help them notice the opening hook of a favorite novel? One of the most famous opening lines in children's literature is the first sentence of *Charlotte's Web*, by E. B. White: "'Where's Papa

going with that ax?' said Fern to her mother as they were setting the table for breakfast." What child isn't instantly awake?
A papa, an ax, all before breakfast? The follow-up line is
equally disturbing. "'Out to the hoghouse,' replied Mrs. Ara-
ble. 'Some pigs were born last night.'" We're not even a hundred words into the novel and everyone *has to keep reading*:
we're worried about the baby pigs!

You might suggest your kids stack a set of ten novels in a
pile. Read each opening line aloud together. Next, rank them
from most compelling to least. Discuss why some books really
pull you in and others don't. This is the kind of literary conversation that fundamentally changes how your kids read—
and then, as a delightful side effect, how they write. They'll
want to have that impact on their own readers. No need to
bludgeon them with a new expectation. The mere conversation of noticing what makes writing interesting will eventually work its magic and influence how your kids compose their
own paragraphs. One eleven-year-old student caught on to
this literary device and launched a story with the following
hook: "The day I almost cut off my finger . . ." Wait, what? We
have to keep reading, right?

How else can we help kids see the power of surprise in
writing? I like to point out surprising comparisons. Gene
Wojciechowski compared a boring basketball game to C-
SPAN—unexpected at the top of a sports article! Similarly, the
following lovely description of a national park by a nine-year-
old includes unexpected comparisons to outer space and an
exotic fruit: "Am I on another planet? The entrance of Joshua
Tree National Park was something out of this world. Trees with
branches as thick as the trunk with sparse, spiky sprouts at the

end of each branch, like the end of a pineapple, were scattered randomly across the flat, desert ground." The comparison to a planet from our solar system and a pineapple in one paragraph keeps me thinking about Joshua Tree in ways I didn't anticipate.

Another tactic for doling out surprises in writing is to do research looking for unexpected facts about the topic. Most kids love to learn fascinating facts that blow the minds of their readers. For instance, one of my ten-year-old students wrote about dolphins and included this interesting fact: "Their head can break your bones in one hit." Even now, reading that fact decades later, I feel my body draw back a bit. Good writing has that effect.

An unusual metaphor captures the attention of readers too. Notice this simile about a piano from Ellie, one of our nine-year-old Brave Writer students: "I have touched every key like a delicate rose petal." The smoothness of a rose petal does, in fact, feel similar to the touch of the ivory keys. This interesting comparison causes me to pause and remember playing piano and pulling the petals off of a rose. Kids are great at drawing out fresh comparisons because they aren't jaded from years of reading clichés. One of our fourteen-year-old students wrote about a baseball game: "I waited for the pitch. I looked at the ball the way a starved man looks at Thanksgiving dinner." This is a player hungry to hit the ball, not intimidated by it. Clever!

Sometimes the best surprises appeal directly to our senses. An eleven-year-old student's report about the Chinese New Year opened like this: "Bing, bang, bam, zing! The fireworks burst into a nighttime rainbow!" Another student—Naomi, eleven—opened her report with sounds too:

Scrape, click. Scrape, click. Scrape, click. The judge tapped his fingernails against the stand in a rhythmic pattern, one after the other. On his left, the jury sat, quietly waiting for the accused to be brought forth. It had been twenty minutes since he'd arrived. Or 1,200 seconds, as he liked to put it.

What I love about the above paragraph is that it includes multiple elements that make me want to keep reading. The sounds at the top appeal to my ears; the presence of a jury indicates a verdict is about to be read, which is enticing all by itself; and the final line cleverly shows how this judge notices the slow progress of time, by measuring twenty minutes in seconds. These details turn this paragraph into a mini movie in my mind.

When we talk to our kids who hate writing, it helps to back up from the act itself and get curious about why we even bother to read, let alone write. Kids need a compelling reason to risk exposing their thoughts to readers (you, teachers, Grandpa). Until they realize that writing can be a source of surprise and intrigue, many of them see the task as tediousness imposed by boring adults! By knowing what some of the tricks are that create surprise, our kids can be guided to write in ways that tickle them.

Why is it that schools forget to include the role of surprise and delight in writing instruction? Because most writing manuals are obsessed with teaching writing formats rather than language play. Formats are not tricky to learn if you already know how to generate language inside yourself and put it on the page or screen. But if you don't have the words yet, and you're instructed to put these imaginary words into a specific shape, writer's block is sure to follow. Most writing manuals that I've reviewed skip the idea of language play completely. They don't deconstruct *good* writing and empower kids to understand how language play works. The emphasis is on tidy writing, not surprising writing. The goal is to produce a clearly worded, correctly described, accurately punctuated and spelled bit of self-expression.

As I have said from the start of this book, I want to shift the criteria for how we evaluate writing from "correct" writing to "compelling" writing. We can't do that if the old methods continue to dominate writing instruction. Part of the trouble is that we offer writing assignments that don't provoke kids to write using their best language and ideas.

PROBLEMATIC WRITING ASSIGNMENTS

The number one complaint I hear from kids about writing assignments is that they're boring. Translation: kids don't care about the topics or formats teachers and curricula assign them. And though they may not think of it in these terms, often a given assignment doesn't help kids produce writing that they know will surprise and delight their reader; that is, it doesn't help them learn how to produce *good* writing. Adults trot out a slew of reasonable reasons why kids need to shut up and do these assignments anyway:

* You won't always get to decide what to write about in high school and college.

* One day, your boss will assign you tasks you don't want to do.

* You're just _____ (fill in the blank: lazy, stubborn, rebellious, etc.).

Please don't say any of these things to your kids. No one was ever motivated to learn because they were shamed into it by someone with more power and authority. These kinds of statements are the bedrock of resentment. Resentment breeds hostility and also, by the way, writer's block or declarations of "I hate writing!"

Remember how your kids learned to talk? Did you give them assignments? Did you expect them to expound on topics that were unfamiliar to them before they were comfortable speaking? Imagine saying to your four-year-old, "I don't want to hear about your miniature cars. Those are toys. One day, you'll need to give an oral report in school. I want to hear an orderly presentation about the importance of brushing our teeth to prevent cavities." Your kids would clam up before they had truly started talking.

There is a wild (and unhelpful) array of writing assignments that teachers and textbooks issue to teach writing. Some programs believe that imagination is the key to learning to write. They assign fictitious scenarios like "An alien visits your school cafeteria. What happens next?" For some kids, this kind of writing prompt may be just the ticket. They love science fiction and storytelling, so they dive in and write. Such kids probably hate the "factual paragraph prompt" about some dull topic like the chief export from the state of Maine. However, for another child—the one obsessed with amassing facts about the real world—a writing prompt about aliens is akin to torture. They *want* to write about the number of toothpicks Maine produces in a year. How can a teacher or parent help a child learn to write when so frequently the topics for writing are a mismatch?

One mom I worked with told me: "My daughter does pretty well with creative writing if she gets to pick the subject matter. She hates it when she's told what to write about. She always thinks that it's a pointless assignment, and since I cringe at my own writing skills, I'm afraid that I'm not much help!"

Another mom shared: "My biggest frustration in teaching writing to my children is their attitude about anything I've assigned them to write. They give the bare minimum amount of effort, and they never proofread. They write just like they talk and don't care about jazzing up the paper. I'll assign them to write in their journals, and they'll write five or six dead sentences. Interestingly enough, though, last summer when I read them *Mrs. Frisby and the Rats of NIMH*, they were so inspired that they each began writing their own sequel to the book. It kept them busy for weeks . . . on their own! How do I get them this excited on a regular basis?"

These are the frustrations and yearnings of so many parents! One of the key ideas in education is this: we learn best when we're interested. Interest allows us to make connections and to retain what we learn. Your child can learn to write using any topic under the sun, just like they learned to speak, talking about any thought that came to mind. Speaking and writing are tools of communication. Fluency in communication depends on practice. This is good news. It means that as the loving, responsible adult in your child's life, you can encourage writing growth independent of the way schools teach it! (Keep reading—this whole book shows you how.)

ASSIGNED WRITING: FRIEND OR FOE?

In fourth grade, my teacher issued a writing assignment to my class. We were supposed to write a few paragraphs in a mini report about a historical figure. She gave us a list of possible candidates for this paper, and I selected Catherine the Great. I did research the way we did it back then: I opened my World Book Encyclopedia to the letter *C* and read about this impressive empress from Russia born in 1729. I didn't have any other sources of information, and my mind was not a treasure trove of facts about Russian royalty either. The few paragraphs in the book would have to be transformed into the paragraphs I wrote for my report. I was ten years old, doing the best I could to paraphrase an encyclopedia.

I thought about my teacher. In my mind, she was about to read a whole bunch of boring reports on plain sheets of lined paper. Since I knew my report wouldn't be very long (I didn't have much to say), I decided to give my teacher a treat. I wrote the report on unlined white construction paper and three-hole-punched it. I put it in a red report folder, secured it with brads, and wrote the report title in big letters on the cover. My cursive sloped because I didn't have lines to follow, but I was proud of my work, and I'd had a great time reading the research, writing the paragraphs, and creating this visual treat for Mrs. Houston.

A week later, the paper came back with the grade C. I had no spelling or punctuation errors, and my content was "good enough," but I was marked down for using unlined paper and putting the report in a folder. According to Mrs. Houston, I had "not followed instructions" and therefore couldn't earn an

A. I was crushed! I had done my best with what limited resources I had to produce surprise and delight in my reader—to produce good writing—but to no avail. It was a lesson in school writing: following the rules was more important than leading from inspiration.

In the world of writing assignments, students can feel as though they're being judged for how well they uphold the criteria of the assignment rather than the writing itself. In many cases, students don't even get the opportunity to showcase their very good writing skills because they're given a truly bad assignment—one that doesn't engage their best ideas, vocabulary, imagination, or interest. What's to be done about these sorts of writing assignments? What makes one assignment a great chance for your kids to grow as writers, and what makes an assignment an impediment to that growth?

The bad news is this: If your kids are in school, they'll have lots of writing assignments, some that they'll hate, and you'll be the one who has to make sure that those assignments get done. If you homeschool, you'll have more control over which writing assignments are used, but you still may have to help your child complete bad writing assignments they get in a co-op or online class.

But the good news is that, even though learning to write based on the criteria in a writing assignment is a worthy skill to cultivate, it doesn't have to be the only writing your kids do. You can give your kids the gift of writing for pleasure, a practice that is essential for a healthy writing life. You get to help your kids learn to write *without* assignments first. There are so many ways to cultivate writing as a natural tool of self-expression outside of the classroom. (See chapter 6 and beyond for those strategies.) My personal preference is to hold off on picky writing tasks until kids are comfortably reading and handwriting or typing. Students are much more able to tweak a writing assignment to suit their particular interests once they feel truly comfortable with the art of writing itself.

What many people don't realize is that you can tweak *any* writing assignment to suit your interests. For example, when I was in college studying history, I would find the aspect of the topic that interested me most. I cared more about social issues, religion, and culture than I did about military strategy, for instance. So if I was assigned to write about the Civil War, I would do my best to orient the prompt to a theme like abolition rather than the South's failed military strategy at Gettysburg. I would suit the assignment to match what was most interesting to me about the overarching topic. Kids can learn to do this from a young age! I'm here to show you how you can help your kids transform any assignment into something approachable and valuable.

REWRITING BAD ASSIGNMENTS

If your kids are being asked to write one of the following terrible, horrible, no good, very bad writing assignments from scratch, it's no wonder they hate writing! Such writing assignments are responsible for damaging countless young writers. Let's look at some of the typical kinds of assignments English programs dole out and how we can transform them from *bad* writing assignments into *good enough* ones! These fixes will help take the pressure off your kids to produce "perfect" writing so they can start finding ways to produce good, surprising writing. Ready?

1. **Write your paragraph on these lines or in this blank space.**

    Worksheets or workbooks that include lines or space for writing on the same page as the assignment can feel intimidating to some kids. They might tense up because it feels like that "official" page is the final version and whatever they write there can't be edited. They don't want to risk making a mistake, so they freeze.

    The fix: Have your child write on scratch paper first. You might even use *real* scrap paper, like the backside of your grocery list. Whatever is written there can be copied over onto the official page later. The writing can go through iterations, removing the high-stakes "one draft" implication of that blank space.

2. **Write three sentences.**

    Lots of assignments tell your kids to write a certain number of sentences. The restriction to three (or five, or twelve) sentences can feel intimidating, particularly if your child loves the topic or has lots to say. They wind up writing three vague statements because the fire hose of detail can't be contained in three sentences.

    The fix: Give your child a chance to get *all* of their words out in a freewriting experience (see chapter 8 for details on how to do this). After the freewrite, take a break from writing. The following day, reread all the sentences and select the most interesting three (or however many) for the assignment.

Experiment with putting the sentences in a variety of sequences before settling on the final arrangement.

3. **Write about your summer vacation.**
    This popular topic is challenging for kids because they're usually *past* summer when they're being asked to write about it. The same goes for writing about the most recent school break or a birthday from a year ago. Kids write best about their direct and immediate experiences. They live in the eternal now. These sorts of topics that ask kids to think back to the past often result in abstract, weak writing. Their impressions are vague. They need a hook—a way to tap into their memories.
    The fix: The first step is to tweak the assignment. Ask a better question: "What is your favorite memory from summer vacation?" or "What was the funniest thing to happen on our summer vacation?" By narrowing the focus of the prompt, you may trigger a specific story the child can retell. Remind your child that the assignment is not meant to be a strict chronology but a retelling of an aspect of it that is the most interesting—whether writing about the amazing roller-coaster ride or the time the car ran out of gas and everyone had to walk two miles to the gas station. To help jog those memories, look at photographs. Have a conversation. Take notes for the child so that they can reference those notes when they sit to write.

4. **Write a five-paragraph essay about X topic.**

If this is the assignment for any kid who is not in high school yet, your child is not really writing an *essay*. They're writing a group of paragraphs about a topic in a report format. Argumentative essays are meant for high school students. Even if the teacher is asking for an "opinion piece," the child is likely writing about their own experiences and thoughts, not citing research to back their viewpoint. So take a deep breath—you can do this without creating a nuclear meltdown.

The fix: The best approach for this kind of daunting writing project is to stop focusing on how the essay should look at the end of the process before you begin. Parents and kids typically want the first draft to be *pretty close* to the final version so there isn't as much mess to clean up. That approach leads to perfectionism and tension.

Instead, you'll need to take a few days for raw bursts of writing that will then get revised into the final form. Start with your child's expertise. Make sure the topic is one that interests your child— tweak it to suit an aspect of the topic your child cares about. For instance, when I was writing with one of my sons about Canada's First Peoples, he got interested when we discovered that lacrosse, a sport he played at the time, was invented by the Haudenosaunee (or Iroquois). That entry point made the whole topic more accessible to him, and he focused his report on the evolution of that game and its role in the community that created the sport.

There are several key ways to create an interesting five-paragraph report or essay for kids under thirteen. Read about the topic from multiple sources and perspectives. Watch related films, if there are any. Visit websites to see images or gather more information. Have a big, juicy conversation about the topic during this research phase. Make a list of facts, stories, expert opinions, and personal experiences on a sheet of paper or on note cards. Then, with the child, pick three key aspects of the topic. Have your child freewrite about each of these aspects in separate sittings on separate sheets of paper (or in different Word documents). Keep the notes on the table for easy reference while writing. Add in quotes or facts. Sort the three paragraphs by importance ("emphatic order" goes from least interesting to most). Add an introductory paragraph that mentions the three key ideas in the next three paragraphs, and close with a concluding paragraph.

You may need to help your child think of transition sentences between paragraphs (a challenging skill for a younger age bracket). The whole process ought to take a few days at least, so be sure to set aside the time. The idea here is to break the task into short, doable chunks over a period of days. Once you have these tidbits of writing, they can be reorganized into the final five paragraphs.

5. **Write about (this specific topic).**
It's tricky to write about a topic that feels irrelevant, unfamiliar, or just plain boring. As I mentioned in

chapter 1, one program I reviewed asked second-grade students to write a descriptive paragraph about a clod of dirt—few kids would find that topic relevant or interesting. The other kind of writing topic that causes kids to freeze is the sort where the only information your child has about that topic is a single paragraph in a textbook. Writer's block is not about the child's unwillingness to write but rather the fact that they don't have enough to say about the subject.

The fix: If there's wiggle room with the teacher, propose an alternate topic. Can the descriptive paragraph be about a mug of hot chocolate or a bottle of perfume rather than a clot of dirt? Can the history assignment be about a person instead of an event? Sometimes kids can be incentivized to write about the topic if they're allowed to change the style of writing—put the event into a comic book format, write a letter exchange between two historical figures, journal a diary entry as the historical figure or as a person who lived at that time, create an advertisement for an invention, write about the topic as a fictional story, compose a review (rather than a book report), and so on.

6. **Write a story about** _____.
   Some kids really hate story-writing. They're "just the facts, ma'am" people. Fun fact: no one *needs* to learn to write fiction. Lots of teachers assume kids prefer storytelling to report writing. In many cases,

they're right. Even so, kids who write stories will draw on their lived experiences in order to write believable tales. Fact-based writing is easiest for most kids, and it's important to know that!

The fix: If your child struggles with fiction, teach them how to *fictionalize* facts by putting them into a story that is true. For instance, you might have your child re-create the moon landing in a story format rather than as a report. Pick a factual event as the basis for that story. Include imaginary dialogue, add a setting, put the events on a timeline so that the child can trace the story chronologically. You might try reading picture books that feature stories of historical figures as a way to model the type of writing your child will do. Research the facts first, and then write the story.

The key to adjusting a writing assignment is to recognize that your child is still *learning* to write. They aren't good at it yet. Some topics or assignments feel more daunting than others! If your child is drawing a blank, tweaking the assignment helps.

You can also try a few of these tips.

* **Look for the surprises.** Think back to what makes writing good and ask the question: *What's surprising about this topic?* Find a surprising aspect of the subject—facts, stories, anecdotes, comparisons. Start the topic in the middle (the cliff-hanging moment), and then, like a movie, retell the story from the

beginning, leading back to that climactic moment. This structure is really popular with kids who enjoy being dramatic!

* **Be sure the child can talk easily about the topic.** If not, do a little more research. Research includes books and websites but also conversations with you, doing the activity (if there is one), watching movies, visiting historical sites (if relevant), looking at artistic depictions of the topic, and so on. The more vocabulary your child has available for the topic, the easier it will be to draft a piece of writing about it.

* **Talk to the teacher.** Sometimes an assignment is just wrong for this particular child. If growing as a writer is the important part of the assignment, see if you can change the topic to suit the child. If the teacher insists on the topic, see if you can switch the format to something less demanding and more interesting to the child (like a comic strip or fictionalized version of the event or an advertisement for the item/invention).

* **Reserve some time for writing that isn't assigned.** If at all possible, write outside of school. This is the kind of writing that some might call "writing for pleasure." Anything from making grocery lists to leaving fun notes for one another around the house counts. Lock-and-key diaries have turned countless kids into writers. New pens and various types of pa-

per (gel pen with black paper is always a winner!) help kids get interested in writing. Try freewriting as a family as well (see chapter 8 for details).

* **Tolerate poor grades in writing.** Try to reduce the pressure to "perform" and focus instead on the process of learning to write, noticing when your kids take writing risks and attempt to put their hearts into writing. Grades usually reflect mechanics more than content, so be the person in your child's life who focuses on the content more than spelling and punctuation.

One last tip: Not every bit of writing a child does has to be revised and edited. Sometimes it's nice to just write for the sake of self-expression or to throw away a piece of writing that didn't turn out the way the child wanted it to. This book is about all the ways you can encourage writing growth as a birthright, not just as a subject in school. A nice side effect is that as your child feels more and more competent in writing, their ability to write well for school grows too!

One of the moms I coached gave me this beautiful description of what happened to her ten-year-old son when she made writing a more natural part of their daily life together: "He grabbed a timer, notebook, and pencil and vanished to a cozy spot by the window. We'd agreed that he'd write for five minutes—but I didn't see him again for over twenty. He told me he just wasn't done when the timer beeped, so he set it for another five minutes . . . several times." Like I've said: when they catch on to the art of writing as self-expression, kids discover that writing isn't so bad after all! What you may notice first is the way their writing gets *good* because you'll be delighted and surprised by some of their choices!

As you've read through these alternate strategies for how to transform a problematic writing assignment into a workable one, I can almost hear you saying back, "But what if my child *just won't write?*" It isn't enough to know what to do if your child is angry and belligerent. You can't grip their fist in yours and move the pencil against their will! The only model of writing instruction most of us have is: "Here's the assignment, follow the instructions, turn in your paper." It can be utterly confounding to see your child dig in and refuse. Parent-student clashes often sound like some version of "Just write three sentences or I won't let you play your video game." Every parent knows that children can outwait any adult when they want to. It's maddening! There is a better way to help your children become comfortable, willing writers. I'm going to show you how to be the supportive writing coach your child needs in the next chapter.

YOUR WRITING ASSIGNMENT

|||||||||||||||||||||||||||||||||||||||||||||||||||||||||||||||||||||||||||||||||||||||||||||||||||

I have two activities for you. First, keep a record of some of your favorite surprising writing that you've read this week. Jot a few of the clever phrases or ideas that caught your attention in a notebook. You can even share these with your kids, but mostly, do it for yourself. Make sure you highlight good writing so that you begin to notice it when it shows up in your children's writing too.

Second, think about the writing assignments your child has been assigned this year (from a homeschool curriculum or from school). Pose the following questions to the assignment and then jot some notes for how to transform it.

» Does it tap into what a child knows well? If not, can you tweak the assignment so that it does? Are any of the child's interests adjacent to this topic?

» Is the topic too vague, general, or outdated? Narrow the focus of the topic by calling to mind a specific experience. Use photographs or images to help jog the child's memory.

» Is it possible to break the assignment into smaller chunks of writing? Instead of writing a complete draft right from the start, identify a few key ideas, facts, or experiences. Write about each one in individual sittings. Put them into a satisfying order and then add an introduction and conclusion.

» If the topic is not familiar to the child, can you find books, films, stories, or websites that grow a child's knowledge base before writing?

» How important is this assignment? Can you skip it? Ask for an extension? Change the format to one the child enjoys, like writing a comic strip or letter or diary entry rather than a report?

||||||||||||||||||||

CHAPTER 6

From Referee to Coach

Whenever I speak to audiences of adults, they nod their heads in warm enthusiasm as I teach. But the moment I ask them to pull out a sheet of blank paper to write for five minutes, the warmth drains from the room and most everyone freezes. They're suspicious. Why are *they* writing? What fresh hell have I introduced into what was a perfectly nice lecture? In that moment, I like to remind parents that this is exactly how their kids feel any time the parent or teacher says: "Time to write!" Children are instantly suspicious: *Why do I need to demonstrate my writing ability? Who will read my writing?*

What if we treated learning to write the way we treat learning to play a sport? Every sport has rules, but no one watches a sports game in order to be amazed by how well a player follows the rules. The rules make the game *playable*, but they're not what make it *interesting*. LeBron James understands the rules of basketball, but it's his talent that makes him a star—

and referees, who understand the rules of play even better than the players do, are not considered skilled athletes. When we think of it in these terms, it seems obvious that kids who want to play a sport usually start with joy in the sport, and *then* they learn the rules of play. Only once they find the sport enjoyable do its rules and techniques begin to hold meaning for them.

What happens if we apply this same line of thinking to writing? Parents often have a hard time coaching their kids to write because they have the wrong objective in mind. They think the game of writing is about crafting perfectly copy-edited text for a letter grade. But as with sports rule books, grammar, spelling, and punctuation are what make the writing *readable*, not what make it *interesting*. Parents taking this approach wind up training their kids to learn the rules of the game before their children experience the thrill of connecting with a reader or playing with language. This is like trying to get kids to idolize referees instead of LeBron.

PLAYFUL MOTIVATION

When I first learned to play tennis as a kid, on day one, the coach told us, "However you can, get the ball over the net." He wanted us to experience the thrill of hitting the ball with a racket to see it go where it could before we put in all the hard work of perfecting our stroke and keeping the ball in bounds. As kids do, we got silly and busy—we tried to hit the ball over the net from between our legs, we put the racket in our nondominant hands, we hit the ball weakly and then chased it while it bounced and bounced to help it to the other side of the court.

As the clinic went on, our motivation to get that ball over the net grew. The coach showed us positions we could take that would improve our chances of hitting that ball where we wanted it to go. This coach wanted us to experience the *joy* of tennis—getting the ball over the net to a waiting player—before we learned how to perform a two-handed backhand with follow-through. This coach saw us as tennis players even before we understood how to serve or keep score. He didn't operate as a referee. He was our ally and friend—our coach!

The trick for most of us in teaching writing, however, is that we've been so conditioned to expect perfect copy, we can't appreciate the child's attempts to connect with a reader. I'll be honest. Whenever I read the raw writing of a child, I wince a little. Every time. It takes discipline to look beneath the messy mechanics to the raw talent or original insight. Adults are put off by inaccurate spelling, missing punctuation, poor grammar, weak phrasing, paltry detail, and messy handwriting. We don't notice the flashes of insight, clever vocabulary, surprising detail, mastery of the material, fluidity of thought, and writing voice. We're too busy being referees instead of coaches. That's why it matters to understand the point of the game first, before we start enforcing its rules.

The question is: Which do we prioritize in teaching kids to write—*accuracy* or *power*? In the game of writing, I believe the goal ought to be *power*—the power to connect to readers. Accuracy is merely a method for ensuring readability to deliver that power.

If a child can toss words around to see what it feels like to play the game of writing, they'll discover the purpose of the game—entertaining readers (including themselves). We can do this at home, playing with writing that's not going to be graded or evaluated by teachers. Once your kids care about communicating their thoughts to readers—you, Grandma, a best friend—they're ready to learn how to support that communication with proper mechanics (the rules or conventions of writing). Too many children have been led to believe they shouldn't play the game called "writing" until they're capable of obeying the rules consistently. We train them to referee their own writing as though being good at the rules for writing is the same as being a skilled writer.

How do athletes become better athletes? They rely on coaches—not referees. Coaches create drills, practice games, and workouts to grow skills and enhance talent. Athletes know that they get to practice their craft without the pressure of playing a game—keeping score, winning and losing. Coaches help players channel their abilities into effective strategies to win the game. Referees are introduced into practice games and mini camps to help players become accustomed to the rules, not to punish players for breaking the rules. By the time the players compete, they have a working knowledge of how to play the game, but they put their focus on being inventive, powerful players who mostly don't break the rules—and when they occasionally do, the referees are there to ensure that the game is played fairly.

If we torture this analogy a little further, we could describe the writing game this way: Kids who understand the goal of writing to be entertaining and informing readers will put their inventive and playful energy toward crafting great language, thrilling stories, and insightful ideas. They'll practice various skills in bursts of writing without having to turn every draft into a finished, edited product. When they do choose to edit a paper and "step on the line" by misspelling a word, they'll be better able to receive the correction by the "referee," because they've already experienced the joy of connecting with a reader.

The next question to ask, then, is: Which do you want to be in your child's writing life—a referee or a coach?

Lots of parents assume their task is to referee the writing because they don't know how to coach it. The irony is that lots of adults aren't all that good at refereeing writing either. Many of us don't know all the uses for a semicolon and can't spell *onomatopoeia* without looking it up. Yet we have enough competence in transcribing our thoughts that we can conduct the writing tasks in our everyday lives without too much difficulty. We use tools like spell check and grammar check—or, in the case of published writing, professional copyeditors—to help us clean up what we haven't mastered. These are the digital and real-life referees that help us turn in a good writing performance.

If you choose to take the role of a coach rather than a referee, you have a better shot at getting a little gratitude (and maybe even a Gatorade bath now and then). Coaches who help their players succeed are well loved, even when their methods sometimes require a pretty tough workout. A coach sees a player's potential and helps the player realize and value it. A coach helps the player understand how to obey the rules while harnessing the player's talents to win the game. A basketball coach might say, "What a long shot, and you made it into the basket! Here's what you can do to avoid putting your toe on the three-point line." In writing, a coach says, "Wow, that sentence delivered a powerful punch of description! Here's how you can punctuate it so that it's easy to read."

FAITH AND FREEDOM

As a coach, you win the loyalty of your kids when you approach them with the twin pillars of writing instruction: faith and freedom. No, I'm not talking about a new political caucus. Faith, in this context, means "Hey, peanut! I know a great writer lives inside your body already. I'm eager to see what's in there!" Freedom means "Of course you'll make a zillion big and little editorial errors on your way to being a great writer. Duh!" The adults in a child's life matter. Your goal is to avoid being the walking, talking red pen that leaves indelible scars on a child's heart.

Take an optimistic posture: a crease-free forehead, a light and breezy tone of voice, a confidence that your child is capable, and an expectation that the writing practices you adopt together will build the skills the writer needs to play the writing game, enjoy it, and win! Winning, in this context, is not a competition with others. It's the risk-taking necessary to connect to readers. In order to put their best thoughts onto the page, our kids need to know we are more interested in their thoughts, first.

One of my first writing students, Rachel—a mother of six—described what it must feel like to have your writing critiqued by your mother.

> Thank you for reminding me that kids need a safe place to put those thoughts and ideas. Writing is sort of like undressing my mind—sometimes it makes me feel downright naked, and it's so crushing to have my poor bare self ogled and poked and critiqued and trivialized instead of listened to. Kids aren't any different

from adults in this, are they? What we put them through in the name of "teaching" is so disrespectful of them as persons. I'm convicted! My daughter has even told me that it hurts her feelings when I point out everything wrong with her writing.

How do we persuade our little charges to trust us to be the kindhearted enthusiasts we promise to be? We commit to *coaching* writers rather than *refereeing* them.

COACH AND PARTNER

Kids need allies—people with power who are on their side when the going gets tough. As the more skilled grown-up, you bring expertise to the table. As the kindhearted adult who loves this child, you provide partnership whenever your child has to learn something new—whether that's using the potty or driving a car. We've already agreed that being the referee in your child's life doesn't necessarily catalyze a passion for writing. But what can a coach do to facilitate that growth? One way to be an effective coach to your child writer is to partner with them as they write.

Picture this: A parent and child are sitting side by side at the table. Each has a piece of paper in front of them. Both hold pencils. Together, they discuss the topic at hand. They each contribute ideas and sentences and new ways to express ideas. Sometimes the parent jots down the child's thoughts. Sometimes the adult encourages the child to write down what they think of together. And sometimes the child jots down their own notes onto their piece of paper without any help at all. Partnering in writing looks like this easy give-and-take while learning the writing process.

Think about it: Isn't partnering how you taught your child to speak? Remember when you pointed to a lamp and said, "Lamp"? Your child said back, "Lamp." Then your child pointed at a hot tub and said, "Chacuzzi." This malaprop entertained you—it didn't unnerve you. Sometimes your child would start down the runway of a sentence and run out of words or conjugations. At that moment, you swooped in to provide the rest, chuckling and rustling the little rascal's hair. The way we treat our kids as they learn to speak is so generous, collaborative, and filled with joy. This can be the experience of teaching a child to write! The whimsy, the partnering, the risks, the loopy leaps in language—writing together can absolutely be as wonderful and stress-free as sharing a conversation.

Travel the road to writing together as collaborators, like a great songwriting team. Think Taylor Swift and Jack Antonoff. This is you with your kid, now. Partnership means doing it together. Like "call and response" or "many hands make light work" or "SpongeBob and Patrick." Collaboration is the name of the game. Some of the writing will be your child's. Some of it will be yours. Some of it will be a delightful amalgamation of your cocreated ideas so tangled you can't tell whose words are whose. In short, as your child's partner in writing, you'll create a patchwork quilt of written words by gathering scraps of language and stitching them together as a team.

Most of the kids who need this level of support are between the ages of eight and twelve. That said, any time a student learns a new writing format (such as essays or research papers), partnering with your child is an effective first step to giving your child the courage to try. My own mother was essential to me in high school when I wrote my first research paper and my college application essay. She walked me through those formats in much the same way she supported me in grammar school. When your child is intimidated by a new writing format, actively partnering with your child is the way to move forward.

To be a partner means to offer support that matches the need. We love to support our kids in all kinds of ways. We boost them up on our thighs so they can wash their hands in a Target bathroom sink. We zip their jackets for them when the zipper gets stuck. We rinse the conditioner out of their hair. We cut their chicken nuggets into bite-sized pieces. We read the instructions to a new game and help them learn how to play it. We show teens how to apply for a job or behave in an interview. We teach them to drive by staying in the car with them. Partnering is so natural to us, we hardly notice that we're being partners to our kids. In fact, parenting could almost be rebranded as "partnering."

Yet somehow we forget the natural assistance we freely offer to our kids when it comes to writing. We may even feel downright guilty for helping them with writing! Why does this old-school viewpoint creep in and make us nervous about offering help to our young writers?

One reason is that many teachers explicitly tell parents *not* to help their kids write. Most teachers have twenty-five to thirty children in their classrooms. They can't know which words in a piece of writing come from the child and which come from the adult. They can't know how much help each parent gave. Teachers worry that an adult will overcompensate for a child's lack of skill and, as a result, they won't get an accurate picture of how well that child can write. If writing is something performed in school and evaluated for a letter grade, this approach has a kind of logic to it.

Unfortunately, by eliminating the parent as a partner, we unnecessarily hamper the child as a writer. Partnering means that when a child encounters a new skill in any area, there's an adult with more experience and confidence handy to support the child's development and to protect them from harm. We would never expect a child to learn to bake cookies by handing them a recipe, ingredients, and free access to the oven. We don't even really use this approach in other school subjects. If your child was struggling with math, you wouldn't worry that it was cheating to hire a tutor. On the contrary, having a hands-on helper give your child the pointers they needed to execute the assignment would be seen as good parenting. I'm here to tell you the same is true for writing. You get to be that "tutor" by partnering with your child. No guilt necessary!

Unlike a schoolteacher, you *do* know how much help you give your child with any process, including writing. You have an accurate picture of where your child still needs to develop or grow and where they shine with confidence and skill. What does that look like in practice?

* You'll recognize which sentence you suggested got included in your child's report.

* You'll know which insight was especially meaningful and needs affirmation.

* You'll be able to identify which words the child can't spell easily.

* You'll be delighted to see the adjectives you brainstormed together show up in the final draft, causing the drab description to suddenly sparkle.

* You'll remember giving a short explanation for why "white house" is lowercased when you're talking about the one in your neighborhood but capitalized when you refer to the one where the president lives.

* You'll recall the conversations you had about the topic that led to that breakthrough in how your child decided to organize their ideas.

Because you're a part of the process, you're also building an internal model of how to help your child grow in their weaker skills. You'll think about how to shore up that lackluster vocabulary or you'll put more energy into practicing certain spelling words. You might realize that one of your children writes best after a long conversation and the other needs to write first and then talk. You might notice that a teen needs lots of access to you during the idea-generation stage and less during the drafting stage, only to need you again when it's time to work on revision.

When you work with your student while they're writing, you're building a coaching relationship—the kind of relationship professional writers have with their editors. There's no shame in it at all. In fact, it's essential and natural in the world of professional writing—writers have editors. When you partner with your child, you're safeguarding your child's delight in writing through collaboration, rather than evaluation.

That said, just about every child (regardless of how kind and supportive you are) will hit a wall where the words won't come. Let's take a look at some strategies to break through writer's block.

WRITER'S BLOCK

In my early forties, I found myself teaching high school students how to write academic essays. I was the owner and creator of Brave Writer, a company designed to teach students to become competent academic writers, ready for college. At the same time, I entered graduate school. When my professor asked us to write research papers, I panicked. It had been twenty years since I had written an in-depth research paper for a grade. What if I earned a B? How could I face my students? Would I deserve to keep teaching high school writing? Suddenly, I feared I was about to find out if I was a fraud. I became cold, clammy, and unreasonably anxious. Every time I began to type, my mind went blank. I would get a few words onto the screen and then delete them immediately. I felt stupid and embarrassed. I was experiencing what can only be described as writer's block.

On one difficult day, it occurred to me that perhaps some of my students might be having similar feelings about writing essays and turning them in for me to read. I decided to share my struggle as a point of empathy. I admitted my worries. I told these thirteen- to seventeen-year-olds what I was going through: "I get what you're feeling! It's awful to worry about how a teacher will receive your writing."

As teenagers do when you trust them with your vulnerability, they swooped in with encouragement and cheerleading:

"You can do it, Mrs. Bogart!" They were boundless in their belief that I would overcome this block. They mirrored back to me the advice I had given them earlier in the class—writing freely, writing about how afraid I was, writing about some other topic first. It was endearing.

I called my professor and spilled everything to her—the source of my anxiety, my fear of the grade she'd give me, the feeling of being a fraud. She listened patiently. She then said, "Julie, what if you write about your anxiety? What if you write a really bad draft and, in it, write about what you fear will happen if you don't get an A on this paper? Can you just write ten pages of worthless words? Perhaps on the other side, you'll finally get to the thoughts and ideas you have inside. I know they're in there." She finished by reminding me that my powers of writing were not on the line. My job was to learn—to explore what I was learning—and she would be my partner in ensuring that I did, in fact, learn what the assignment was meant to teach me.

It was eerie. She gave me the advice I had given to all my students—the same advice my students had just given to me. It was advice I knew well, but in my greatest moment of panic, I couldn't imagine that it would save me. And so, with the support of several teenagers and a professor with a PhD, I sat down in the library the next day with my computer open and banged out ten pages of all of it: my ideas, my fears, my thoughts about the readings, my negative self-talk about my academic skills, a long-winded personal story that barely related to the topic—everything. When I was finished, I printed it all. I read it. And I threw it away. The next day, I started over and wrote my paper.

I learned an important lesson. Whether you're six, sixteen,

or forty-six, writer's block comes for all of us. If we don't have a safe space in which to talk about it and risk writing badly, it's really difficult to shake. When kids find it challenging to even move the pencil, too often the adult who cares about them shifts from coach to referee—and then to judge. Adults are quick to tell kids that their protests and complaints are excuses for shirking their responsibility to do the assignment. We judge our kids as having weak moral character, believing they're lazy or defiant rather than offering them strategies to help them get out of the awful feeling of not having the words available for writing.

The nature of writer's block has been dissected by scholars, educators, and authors for centuries. The upshot of their analysis is that most everyone at some point in their writing lives will experience writer's block, even professional writers. It's an ordinary feeling—nothing to cause alarm.

But being told something is normal doesn't make it go away. We all know it's normal to feel nervous during a stage performance, but that doesn't stop you from sweating while giving a speech. Think of all the times you've felt stymied by the writing experience. Whether it was a challenging paper topic in college or an email to your soon-to-be ex-husband about your divorce or the carefully worded letter to customer service—sometimes the stakes in writing are so high you lose your nerve—and then your words.

Yet when kids don't want to write, or when they get stuck and can't think of what to put on the page, we often attack their character. We don't think about the fact that they're going through the same experience many professional writers and adults know well. Parents have a habit of attacking a child's character when they can't think of a better way to help their kids out of tricky feelings. Truth be told, writer's block has nothing to do with character. It's a benign and infuriating condition most creatives face.

To write freely, a writer needs three conditions to be present.

1. They need room for risk, exploration, and revision.
2. They need to know a lot about the topic (enough to talk about it over pie with a friend).
3. They need to feel comfortable with the format (the container for the writing).

If any of these is missing, you can bet your child will start swinging their legs under the table and picking a fight with the toddler. They may not know how to tell you they're blocked, but trust me, when kids have safety, an abundance of words, and a feeling of competence in writing, they write.

REASONABLE KIDS

When coaching kids, let's start with the idea that any problem they express is reasonable. I know that may sound absurd, since children are not always rational in their self-assessment. They have limited experience and skill. They might say "I hate writing" when they really mean "I'm hungry." But if we take them at their word, we can start by investigating "I hate writing" and help them work backward until they discover that what they were really feeling was the need for a turkey sandwich. Everything we need to know to help our kids is hiding behind their blunt attempts at expressing their distress.

We can begin by showing interest in their resistance.

"You hate writing? Tell me more about that. What do you hate about it?"

"Your hand hurts? Show me where. I see. Let's massage that finger a bit and take a break."

"You think the topic is stupid? What's stupid about it to you? Have you ever thought about explaining why the topic is stupid in writing? That could be an interesting paper."

"You hate sitting at the table? Would you be interested in writing on a clipboard on the couch? What about sitting under the table instead?"

"Writing is hard? Yeah, I think it is, too, sometimes. I can remember a time when it was hard for me. What makes it hard for you?" (Then take notes so that they see you taking their complaints seriously.)

"You don't like writing when you can't spell every word correctly? So annoying. I get it. I wonder what I can do to help you with that. Let's brainstorm. Maybe call out a word when you need the spelling, and I can write it on the whiteboard for you to copy."

"You thought you hated writing, but you just feel annoyed by it? Hmm. Do you think you feel hungry, bored, tired, or antsy? Maybe we can eat a snack outside while we play with the dog and then try again."

"There's too much to say, so you can't think of anything to write? Let's pull out my phone and do a little voice-to-text to capture your many amazing thoughts. Then we can reorganize them. Want to?"

The goal here is to validate what your child says, offer a corresponding experience if you have one, and then consider ways to address whatever the problem is. One of my kids couldn't work on writing during the day because he was a born birder and watching birds through our window was too distracting. For a few weeks, we shifted our writing time to the evenings so the windows would be dark. Problem solved!

When we talk about writer's block, we're talking about the legitimate feelings your kids have, even if those feelings are inconvenient and seem small to you, the adult. When we take our kids seriously (even if what they express doesn't quite make sense to us), we have the best chance of overcoming the block! In the next few chapters, we're going to look at the specific strategies that unlock our young writers. I've offered you a slew of ideas, but feel free to pick and choose. Take your time. Some of them will be wildly freeing and others will fall flat. That's okay! Your job is to be a detective to discover what tool helps propel your child into writing *today*.

YOUR WRITING ASSIGNMENT

Describe a time when writing deserted you. How did you cope? What helped you break through writer's block?

|||||||||||||||||||||

Writing Back

*Y*ou have strong muscles.
 Today's weather will be 57° F.
There's a new egg in the robin's nest! Have you seen it?
Peter Piper picked a peck of pickled peppers. Can you say that three times fast?
4 × 6 = ? Do you know?
I love how you shared your crayons with your sister yesterday. That was generous.
What do you want for lunch?
Let's play Settlers of Catan this afternoon.

Picture writing each of the above statements on a colorful sticky note in a variety of marker colors. After your young child goes to sleep, you creep into their bedroom and plaster these notes all over the inside of their door in a big array at their eye level. On the ground, at the base of the door, you leave a stack of sticky notes and a marker.

What will happen when your child wakes up in the morning? Will they be startled? Will they try to read what's there? Of course! Between facts, compliments, equations, and questions, your child is being invited to engage with writing. They may call for you. You'll help them read the notes. They may need a little support with words like "pickled" and "generous." Or maybe they're working on their times tables and 4×6 stumps them. What will they do next? Will they write their own notes to you on the stack of sticky notes you left for them? Will your door be peppered with questions and doodles and notes the next morning?

If you want a child to write, provoke them into it! Assignments feel like chores, but tiny squares of words in colorful markers on a door as the publishing surface? Sign them up! They love it! In fact, they'll want to "write back." Safeguard your child's pleasure in writing and your child will grow as a writer.

To try this practice with your young writers, here's what you need to do!

* Purchase lined sticky notes in a variety of colors.

* Collect sayings, tongue twisters, jokes, famous quotes, compliments for your child, the weather report, fun facts, and so on.

* Jot one item on each note.

* After your child goes to bed, stick the notes at eye level on your child's bedroom door.

 ⋆ Leave a couple stacks of sticky notes plus pens at
 the base of the door for your child.

 ⋆ See what happens!

Naturally, if you have a lot of kids, you may need to populate multiple doors with notes! No one wants to be left out. Try
it on a weekend when there's lots of time for them to respond.
Kids are more likely to write if they're provoked into it—or, we
could say, *invited* into it. The key to a vibrant writing life is the
feeling that you've *got* to write because someone, somewhere,
needs to hear what you have to say. We feel the most motivated
to write when we're "writing back"—that is, responding to the
provocation to write.

This is actually the entire premise of social media! I like to
say to parents (as a way to shock them with truth) that my best
student writers have been the ones with a lot of access to the
internet. Why? Because these are the kids who write to entertain and connect with readers. They're obsessed with writing
back. They see the comment sections of their favorite online
spaces the way they might see these sticky notes on a door: as
invitations to put their thoughts in writing too.

If you've got tweens or teens, take advantage of whatever
text messaging system your family uses instead of (or in addition to) their doors. Your kids may or may not have a cell
phone. That's okay! You can use any number of apps that make
it easy to connect digitally. Try sending your teen a link to an
article related to their favorite topic. Ask them a question that
relates to an area of expertise. Send them a joke or an interesting quote from a book you're reading that reminded you of

them. Ask for their interpretation of a lyric from a song they know well. The key is to provoke them into *writing back*. Lots of tweens and teens find the texting format to be low stakes and irresistible. Use it to your advantage!

The urge to write back is similar to the volley and response of conversation. We love to talk with someone. When someone says a statement or expresses an opinion, we are automatically invited to participate and self-express. Before you can expect kids to automatically participate in a written exchange, it helps to gin up the back-and-forth impulse through oral conversation. When you're learning to write well, it helps to be good at talking, reading, and conversing!

WRITING OFF THE PAGE

So much growth in writing happens *off the page*. We seed our kids' imaginations with all kinds of interesting ideas, facts, opinions, and stories. Kids are more likely to write freely and well if they have conversations with interested adults; follow instructions to build, bake, or backpack; role-play in dress-up clothes; read a wide variety of books; watch television shows; debate ideas; participate in the arts; walk in nature; develop hobbies; and play sports. Why? Because when you invest in living a rich life, you have lots to express to others! People build their vocabularies in specific domains through immersive experiences. It's difficult to write from a dry well. Kids who lead fulfilling lives will have lots to write about. Children who are all work and no play? Not so much. When your child is stuck, stuck, stuck, sometimes the best thing you can do is get up from the table and dive into a language experience with them—anything from reading aloud to attending a play to building a LEGO set.

In fact, even television and movies can be incredible sources for vocabulary development—way better than workbooks! You may balk at this idea, but hear me out. The most talented actors are given a script written by professional writers. The actors are directed to perform those words for the greatest comedic or dramatic impact. The actors' entire job is to ensure that the viewer understands both the meaning of the words *and* how those words advance the story. If you want children to develop their vocabulary, put the words in the hands of an actor every time. Popular entertainment is entertaining for good reason. Sitcoms and cartoons, Disney movies and PBS documentaries, audiobooks and songs deliver so much more than we give them credit for. My kids have even told me that some of their most memorable bits of historical trivia have come from watching *Friends* or *Seinfeld*, when an offhanded remark or joke made them curious about the causes of World War I or the controversy surrounding JFK's assassination.

Your young writers will grow *off the page* if they . . .

* Have conversations with you over dinner, in the car, at night before bed, and so on.

* Read (including both audiobooks and reading to themselves).

* Stroll through the library stacks, especially when looking at book titles in an area of interest.

* Draw, paint, and sculpt.

* Go for a run, play soccer, tumble on a gymnastics mat, practice yoga, or shoot hoops—any sport where they connect to the direct experience of using their bodies and growing the domain-specific vocabulary that goes with it.

* Watch television and films of a variety of genres, including fantasy, documentaries, reality TV, biopics, sports, science fiction, novels turned into movies, period pieces, and comedies.

* Attend plays (including Shakespeare!).

* Enjoy poetry by reading it aloud with family or friends.

* Listen to podcasts and music (consider following along with the lyrics for added value).

* Play board games, dice games, and video games.

* Sew a quilt or build anything with instructions—computers, birdhouses, IKEA furniture, LEGO bricks, model airplanes.

* Walk in nature, particularly while using a field guide, binoculars, and a magnifying glass, during a variety of times of day, in every season of the year.

* Visit an art museum, picking a style or era and learning about it.

How do these activities contribute to the writing life, you ask? There's an old saying in professional writing that gets quoted frequently to novice writers: *Write what you know.* The idea is that you can't write about a topic you don't know well enough. Sure, a student can be assigned a topic for writing, but if they haven't put in the time to get to know that topic thoroughly, writing will feel like a chore. If you ask a child to write about a video game they love and play every day, you'll get rich vocabulary and vivid detail. They'll be able to sequence the steps with precision.

If you ask the same child to write about the planet Venus after reading one paragraph in a textbook, your child may stare at you blankly, saying they can't think of anything to write—which would be true. All the good words were used up in that one paragraph. They haven't got enough depth or breadth in the topic to contribute anything new in their own writing. Students who are assigned topics in school often wilt in the face of the daunting task of writing because they truly can't think of enough words to say about the subject.

When we ask our kids to write, one of the first questions to pose to ourselves should be: "How well does my child know the topic?" Our job is to then find experiences to go with that subject matter in order to expand the child's reservoir of language and ideas. Taking Venus as our example, ask yourself, "How can I make that writing project more relevant?" If you have time, by all means, visit an observatory or talk with a local astronomer. If you're in a time crunch, look at images and videos online. Stay up late and find Venus in your own night sky. Conduct an online search to learn about the origin of the planet's name. Read multiple nonfiction accounts of the solar system, in books and on websites. Find poetry or artwork centered on Venus. Once your child has thought about Venus in a variety of ways and has corresponding experiences, they'll be more capable of launching into that first draft.

Even with a deep dive into the topic, it can be difficult to download all those words in one gush from your brain to the page. Sometimes it helps to start with what I call a "big juicy conversation." Give your child a chance to put that research and experience into oral language in a natural exchange of ideas, facts, and details with you. Your task is to learn how to ask the right kinds of questions to draw out what your child knows. This early step in the writing process is key. You're developing your child's capacity to put their vague thoughts into specific language.

The next step is to shrink the writing task to address a single aspect of the topic, one at a time. Your child will not write about "Venus" in general but about the planet's location in the solar system in one sitting, who discovered the planet and how in another sitting, and what the child noticed when they looked at Venus through a telescope in another. After three days, your child will have three bits of writing that pertain to the overarching topic. By reducing the size of the writing assignment to aspects of the subject prompted by well-crafted questions, you help your child right-size the project into components rather than expecting a complete first draft with all the information the child knows sorted and organized.

When teaching writing to a child who is reluctant or resistant, I recommend sticking first to topics the child knows and loves. Writing can be taught with *any* subject matter. Writing about a topic the child doesn't love is a next-level skill. Start with what your child already knows. Let them show off their expertise and their well-developed vocabulary in that domain. Use that beloved topic to teach them how to find their words—how to access all that language and experience that lives inside them—and then how to revise and edit. Once this practice becomes natural and comfortable, they'll be more able to apply those same skills to a writing assignment from school.

THE PODCAST MODEL

Imagine being invited on a podcast or talk show as a guest. You have an area of expertise the host values and wants to share with their audience. You come ready to have a conversation. When you mic up, however, the host simply introduces you to the listeners and says, "Please share with our audience everything you know about [insert area of expertise]." How would you feel? A little blindsided? Would you wonder what the host hoped you'd share and if you were on the right track? Could you keep going without any conversation or prompting? What if the host stayed silent when you ran out of stories or new ideas? Wouldn't you get a little desperate to find out if you were living up to the host's expectations? Perhaps you'd be tired from monologuing and want a break. At minimum, wouldn't you want a few questions to keep you going?

I've been on countless podcasts. I can talk fairly easily for long periods of time. But if the host isn't actively engaged with what I'm sharing, I start to wonder if I'm off target. I feel abandoned. A two-way conversation helps me find language I didn't even know was inside. Questions trigger memories and information I would not access otherwise. When we use language to express ourselves (orally or in writing), we're seeking connection with a person on the other side of that communication. We lose heart if we go on too long alone or don't get feedback that helps us refine the message. Sometimes we miss valuable ideas because we didn't have the right prompt to draw them out.

Writers under the age of eighteen are sometimes treated like they're in solitary confinement. Adults act as though writing has to happen in isolation, without human contact, or it doesn't count. Yet for the novice writer in particular, this can be a demoralizing and panicky experience. It feels a lot like going on a podcast and monologuing without any way to know if the audience is still listening. One of the best ways to support your young writer, then, is to participate in their writing experience by interviewing them about the topic. The questions you pose shouldn't be a rapid-fire interrogation. In fact, it's great to start with a free-wheeling conversation. Have it naturally in the car or while you clean up the dinner dishes.

As you notice that your child is getting comfortable with the topic, you can pivot to using these questions and prompts for writing—just as we discussed with the Venus example. I recommend that you ask a question, discuss it for a few moments, and then have your child write about just that aspect of the topic for two to three minutes. These bursts of writing about very specific aspects of the topic help your child narrow their focus so that they can generate thoughts to write on the page. If you continue this way, your child will have lots of paragraphs to shape into a final, coherent document. But let's not get ahead of ourselves—we'll discuss more of that process in chapter 9 when we look at revision and editing. Before we get there, let's look at the type of questions to ask, how to use a practice called freewriting, and some tools for playing with revision. If you dedicate unhurried time to each of these processes, your reluctant writers will come out from behind the curtain and take a few writing risks.

PODCAST HOST

Previously, I had you imagine you were a guest on a podcast or talk show. Now I want you to think of yourself as the host and your child as the guest. What can you ask your child about a topic that will provoke deeper reflection and bursts of language? You're not quizzing your child as much as interviewing them. Your goal is to uncork their expertise. Your child should feel pumped up by the questions you pose, not evaluated and found wanting.

Great questions are open-ended. In fact, the best questions will elicit responses you can't predict in advance. Kids who are asked high-quality questions feel valued, want to show off what they know, and are usually quick to respond. Sure, some introverts may be less verbose in their replies. But most children really enjoy being seen as the expert. They like the feeling of competence that being able to answer questions gives them. Pause for a moment and really take this in. Many times, when kids clam up, it's because they feel trapped or tricked or truly don't have the information you expect them to have. They think they're being tested, even when the adult has tried to reassure them that's not the goal.

If you want your child to take pride in what they know, you can prime the pump by expressing what you don't know first. Show your ignorance. Ask a question that guarantees the child's expertise is essential to help you learn. By the way, sometimes the question process will reveal that the child still doesn't have enough information about the topic. That's a sign that you and your child need to go back to reading and immersive activities before writing.

I've grouped some possible questions you can ask into a few categories. You can borrow these and tweak them to suit a particular topic. I hope they inspire you to come up with your own too!

Questions About Significant People

These questions will help your child explore information about a historical figure, artist, scientist, author, poet, or other important person.

1. Imagine that you like this person. What do you like about them?
2. Imagine that you dislike this person. What do you dislike about them?
3. Picture this person at a party. How would they behave and why?
4. Where did this person grow up? How did their childhood home influence their life's work?
5. Who might play this person in a movie? Why?
6. What character in a book does this person remind you of most and why?
7. How would you describe this person's contribution to their field? Are we better or worse off because of it? Why?
8. Who are the important people in this person's life? Why are they important?

9. Does their physical appearance relate to the key achievements in their life? If so, how?
10. Imagine the world without this person's contribution. How would our lives be different?

Questions About Places

Questions like these will help your child think about planets, countries, cities, natural sites, historic sites, factories, buildings, domestic dwellings, and any other type of place.

1. Imagine being in this place. What do you see? What sounds do you hear? What temperature is it? What fragrances and odors do you notice? Put yourself there as best you can.
2. Who would you take with you to visit this place? Why? What would you expect that person to see, feel, say about it?
3. How does this place rank among other similar places? For example, is it the biggest, coldest, tallest? Is it similar to another more or less well-known place? Is it well known for one aspect and not as well known for another?
4. What type of person might like to visit this place?
5. Can you describe the physical composition of this place? What are its key features?
6. If you were to paint this place in a painting, what style of artwork would you choose? Impressionistic? Realism? Surrealism? Anime? Why?
7. Can you list as many facts as you know about this place? Think about size, atmosphere, population (if

there is one), animals, natural elements, and anything else you know.

8. Why do you think this place matters? To whom is it important?

9. Who are the experts that talk about this place? What are two opinions they have about it?

10. If people live there, who are they? What are their daily habits? What religion or government do they have?

Questions About Hobbies and Experiences

Dig into your child's thoughts and feelings about sports, creative pursuits, leisure activities, and talents with these questions.

1. What makes this hobby or experience pleasurable?

2. Who does it best? What kind of person isn't suited to it?

3. If you were to explain the process to someone, how would you describe what a person with this skill does?

4. What's one time when you struggled with this skill?

5. What's another time when it all clicked?

6. Can you take me into your experience? Can you show me how this experience looked, felt, and became meaningful to you?

7. What's the history of this talent or hobby?

Questions About Literature

After reading short stories, books, and other literature, use these questions to explore what you've just read with your child.

1. What is the most memorable scene that you can recall right now? Why?

2. Did this book hook you right from the start, or was it a slow burn? How and why?

3. Which character do you relate to the most? Which one the least? Why?

4. Did you care about what happened to the main character? Why or why not?

5. If you could interview the villain in the story, what questions would you ask and why?

6. Did you enjoy the world this story is set in? What about that world is inviting? What about it is alienating?

7. Who's your favorite side character? Would you want to be friends with that character? Why or why not?

8. What problem did the ending solve? How did the ending strike you? Satisfying? Annoying?

9. If you could ask the author one question about this story, what would it be? What would you hope to hear? What would be disappointing to hear?

Questions About Film

Movies are a great way to grow a child's capacity to analyze stories. You might try our family trick of holding the remote control and pausing the film once in a while to pose questions like these.

1. A few minutes after the movie begins: Who are we rooting for? Who are we rooting against? How do we know who we should root for?

2. After a sequence that relies heavily on the musical score: How does the music influence our mood while viewing? How would this scene feel without the music?

3. Mid-movie: What has to happen for this movie to end? What do you hope the ending will be? What ending would be unacceptable to you? Which do you think it will be? Why?

4. Most of the way through the film: Has your opinion about any of the characters changed since the beginning of the film? Which characters and why?

5. At the end: Did you guess the ending? Are you happy with it? Why or why not? If you imagine that a follow-up movie could be made after this one, what would be the story based on where these characters are at the end of this film?

You may think of other questions now that you've read these. The goal is to pose questions in a natural conversation over donuts or hot cocoa. Take notes. Hand those notes back to your child and invite them to write about a few of their responses—the ones that catalyzed the most conversation. I recommend that the child keep these notes on the table next to them as they handwrite or type. They can refer to the notes when they get stuck or need to remember the ideas that were meaningful to them. Sometimes your child will do better answering the questions in a document on a laptop or iPad. Put the questions in bold and let them type their answers below. Remember: kids love to "write back," so make the questions provocative. State an obvious untruth or put some emotion into the question. You might even include your own personality: "Were you as annoyed by the ending of the book as I was? How would you have wanted the book to end?" This kind of question provokes a response!

Some writing assignments come with a series of questions embedded in them. In a similar way, the student can talk with you about them first, and then write about each one, one at a time. The goal is to generate way more writing than is needed for the final draft. When kids discover that they have a lot to say (an abundance of thoughts!), writing becomes less daunting. When they feel the engagement of an interested "host" (you), they're more likely to want to entertain or inform you. Most of us are happy to write back when we feel that the other party wants to know what we have to say. Look at social media! It is entirely built from the premise that everyone wants to write back.

You may be wondering how to get a good first draft out of this collection of bits and pieces of writing. You may say, "Julie, that's all well and good. My kid can write a draft, but when I try to offer revision advice, our entire relationship blows up!" I hear you! That's what we're about to tackle in the next chapter.

YOUR WRITING ASSIGNMENT

Think about a time on social media where you felt compelled to "write back." Imagine the scenario and the feeling that drove you to respond. Write a bit about that. Now imagine offering that opportunity to your child!

‖‖‖‖‖‖‖‖‖‖‖‖‖‖‖‖‖‖

CHAPTER 8

The Joy of Messy Writing

When I was eleven years old, I handed my mother my rough draft of a short story about an American girl who got separated from her family while on vacation in Mexico. My mother read my draft eagerly with a smile on her face. She recognized the details from our recent family trip to Guaymas. She laughed and showed concern at the right spots in the story. When she finished, she gave me the compliments I craved. It felt good to be *read*. Then she offered an observation: "I notice at the beginning of your story, you *tell* the reader about packing for the train trip. I wonder if you can hook the reader right away. What would you think about adding a bit of dialogue and activity at the start?"

I hadn't considered that. My story read more like a summary in a diary than action that could be seen in the mind of the reader. My mother suggested, "Let's act it out. You play the main character, and I'll play your sister. What kind of conversation would we have as we pack for the train trip to Mexico?"

We got out of our chairs. My mother led the way by starting a pretend conversation. I responded naturally, improvisationally. Then it was her turn, and she made another comment. I replied. We put pretend clothes into pretend suitcases. Back and forth we went. Once we had explored all the possible ways to talk about packing and preparing for the trip, my mom said, "That was great! Let's get it on paper before we forget." Much scribbling and revising ensued.

We worked through the rest of my story, adding bits of detail, dialogue, and action using a similar approach. By the end, there was a big batch of margin notes I could choose to incorporate into the final draft—or not! It was up to me. What I'd learned, however, is that readers like writing that pops. I wanted to have that effect, so I was eager to apply my mom's ideas. All of it felt fun and interesting. Later that day, I grabbed my favorite purple pen and a yellow report folder. I rewrote the opening and made some additions to other sections based on my conversations with my mom. I handed in my story to the teacher, wondering how it would be received. She loved it!

When I look back at how my mother worked with me, I'm touched. I never felt critiqued. I don't remember wishing she'd stop. I wasn't nervous. I didn't feel threatened or invalidated. I liked playacting with her. I felt supported. In fact, I learned a lesson I've never forgotten. You've got to hook the reader right away. The best writers drop right into the action or start with dialogue or express a surprising statistic. I was lucky. My mother, a professional writer, has an abundance of enthusiasm for and confidence in the writing process. Her approach to my writing over the years has been a steady source of warmth and practical feedback that feels supportive, never critical or condescending. I, in turn, loved writing and knew I could do it!

What would it be like for your child to see writing as this freewheeling, playful collaboration? It absolutely can be. The key to learning to write is to create space for freedom and play, both in writing and in the initial stages of revision. Let's do that now.

FREEWRITING FUNDAMENTALS

There's no injunction that says you can't write unless all your grammar and spelling ducks are in a row. Where did we get this wild idea? It's nutty! I remember that I won the spelling bee in fourth grade. As an adult, I have often prided myself on my knack for good spelling. One day I was digging through a box of memorabilia and found my fourth-grade diary. It was riddled with misspellings! It occurred to me that perhaps I was merely a good speller *for fourth grade*. That was a revelation! My diary proved that I was a growing speller who also felt free to write anyway. To grow as a writer, it's important to create room for lots of writing that is subpar, doesn't match a format, and comes willy-nilly from our insides without all that self-critique and evaluation. In other words, your kids get to throw away a lot of writing on their way to being competent, confident writers!

The little-known secret of published authors is how many thousands of words never make the cut or see the light of day. I just looked at my "writing leftovers" document where I store the words I've cut from this book's first draft so far: 27,337 words. Yes, there are currently nearly 30,000 words that you'll never read—that's about half of a full-length book!—sitting in a document that were removed from the working draft of this book. That's typical of most freelance writers. They write and they write and they write, and a little of it makes it to publication. Yet somehow students are under the impression that they've got to cough up the exact right number of words that are perfectly spelled, organized, and well-argued on their first attempt to put their thoughts in writing. It's madness!

As an adult invested in your child's success, you have the chance to reverse the curse. Let's help our kids slather pages and screens with scads of words that no one has to edit or read or fix or correct. Let's give our kids pure freedom to jot down the wild array of thoughts that live in their minds—unedited! One of my great writing-instruction heroes, Dr. Peter Elbow, coined the term "freewriting" to describe this unfettered approach to learning to write.

Freewriting is the practice of writing without thinking about writing, the same way we talk without thinking about talking. Read that again. Freewriting means writing without paying attention to typing or handwriting skills, or remembering which way the *d* or *b* goes. It means the writer can toss out any spelling without worrying about getting it right—they put all their attention on their thoughts and write them exactly as they come. The only goal in freewriting is to keep the pencil moving for a predetermined amount of time. Freewriting trains the brain to hook up with the hand so that the ticker tape of thoughts running through the mind filters down through an arm to the pencil or keyboard and onto the page or screen. The hand and the brain form a friendship where the hand is merely taking dictation from the mind.

Why is this stage of growth in writing so critical? Because freewriting teaches a child how to write at the pace of thought.

Freewriting is the foundation of all writing formats—fiction, nonfiction, all of it. In fact, I'd argue that freewriting is the bedrock practice for a vibrant, healthy writing life. Freewriting is a tool that everyone ought to have in their tool kit. It helps with exploring a topic, generating insight, breaking out of writer's block, and even healing emotional pain. Freewriting can also be used in academic writing: to generate a first draft, to make ideas more precise, to identify the language of a counter-argument, to play with summary and paraphrasing, to integrate data into an existing draft, and to compose essays and research papers.

What sets freewriting apart from other kinds of writing is that it depends on an arbitrary set of rules (keep the pencil moving for a certain amount of time, writing whatever comes to mind) that support the exploration of a child's thoughts in writing. These rules are not performance-based the way they are when you start with an outline or try to follow a format. Rather, freewriting gives the student a container for self-expression that liberates the child to tell the truth while paying little attention to how those words show up on the page or screen.

In the previous chapters, I urged you to jot down your child's words on their behalf before they could read and hand-write fluently. As they grow in their reading and handwriting skills, they benefit from partnering with you in the next phase of their development as writers. Once they get good at writing with you, your kids are ready to take up the pencil or keyboard for themselves, on their own. Freewriting is the practice that ushers your child into greater independence in writing.

I recommend that everyone in the family freewrite together—including the adults. As I've mentioned, one of my favorite writing coaches, the late Pat Schneider, said that everyone ought to take the same writing risks together. She urged a democracy of writing. In this way, we get rid of the expectation of a performance for evaluation and instead invite everyone to grow as writers. There's something transformational that happens when the adult caregiver or teacher experiences the same thrill of anxiety about writing as the kids in their charge.

"I THINK I CAN, I THINK I CAN"

I remember one Brave Writer mother with very unhappy writers in her family. She felt a bit desperate to turn things around. I recommended she try freewriting weekly with her two girls, without any other kind of writing activity, for eight to ten weeks. They lived in Europe, and once a week, they took a train to another city for an appointment. The mother decided this train ride would be an ideal setting for freewriting. So, each week, the three of them wrote silently on the way to their appointment and then read their freewrites aloud to each other on the way back. Within a few weeks, the girls were hooked. What had been a dreaded task became the highlight of the weekly trip. Freewriting completely transformed how her girls felt about writing—they saw it as part of an adventure that they shared, not as a school assignment to drum out for a grade.

The mother told me that she, too, understood writing in a brand-new way. She got nervous to share her writing aloud with her girls because she felt like she didn't have anything of merit to "say." But her daughters supported her enthusiastically, just as she did each of them. In a year's time, these girls went from hating writing to writing in their free time at home!

This mother was amazed. I was not—I've seen it happen so many times now that I know it's possible to transform the writing culture in your family simply through a regular free-writing practice. The genius of freewriting is that you and your kids can freewrite anywhere—like in a coffee shop or at the library or outside at a picnic table.

> A caveat: there are some students who don't like writing to a timer. In that case, simply suggest freewriting for half a page or until they run out of words. Some kids feel nervous about writing with their siblings present. That's okay too. Have that child try writing in the evening just with you or writing alone in their bedroom to see how it goes. You can always modify any practice to suit your child. The key to building up that writing muscle is simply to write without fear of making mistakes and to do so regularly.

FREEWRITING GUIDELINES

Below are what I consider the most important guidelines for a successful freewriting practice. Be sure to share them in your own words with your kids. It helps to have a snack ready to eat once the timer dings!

* **Kids can write about a topic they love or simply whatever comes to mind.**
  Some kids benefit from having a topic to write about and some need total freedom. The day before the first freewrite, have your kids make lists of the stuff

they love and know a lot about. On the day of the freewrite, they can either pick a topic from the list *or* write whatever comes to mind (or a combination of both)! Sometimes what comes to mind is that they don't like freewriting or can't think of anything to write. That's okay! Welcome all those words too.

* **Set a timer for an agreed-upon amount of time.**
For beginners, start with three minutes. Over the course of several weeks, increase by thirty seconds each week as your kids feel ready. Ask them if they want more time. The goal is to eventually be able to freewrite for about ten minutes (but know that it could take a year or more to get there). For high school students, building up to thirty or forty minutes is a great goal; timed freewriting prepares them for in-class essay writing.

* **Keep the pencils moving the entire time until the timer dings.**
Remind your children to write everything that comes to mind, even seemingly unrelated comments like "I hate writing. This is too hard. I don't care about American history." Some kids prefer freewriting on the computer. That's okay too, but be sure to include some handwritten freewrites as well so that both typing and handwriting skills get practice.

* **No self-editing.**
Let them know you aren't going to correct their writing. It's okay if they have messy handwriting,

poor spelling, grammatical errors, sentence fragments, lists of verbs, and repeated words. Tell them to get it all down without worrying about how it looks, the order of the thoughts, or whether or not the writing is punctuated and spelled accurately. If they get stuck, they can write "I'm stuck, I'm stuck" or they can move to another line on the page or re-state the topic for writing. That restatement often jump-starts a lagging mind.

* **Be outrageous.**
They are free to use vocabulary and descriptions that sound overboard, silly, or absurd. Let them know that they can make comparisons and connections to other subjects (even if those connections seem, at first glance, to be irrelevant or unrelated). Keep writing, no matter what, until the bell rings, and then stop.

* **Celebrate!**
High fives all around. Admire the pencil marks on that sheet of paper! Let them know you're glad they wrote.

Additional guidelines can include:

* **Freewrite together once a week.**
A weekly freewriting practice *is* enough! I like Fridays because of the alliteration (Friday Freewrites), but I hear Wednesdays or Sundays work just as well (wink).

✳ **Give each writer an opportunity to read their writing aloud—but only if they want to.**

I recommend no one read their freewrites aloud on the first week so that everyone has a sacred, private writing space. Then, the second week and following, offer the chance to read aloud without making it a requirement. Consider going first as a role model. Reading aloud is a wonderful way to normalize that everyone has thoughts worth expressing and hearing. Your only task when listening to a freewrite read-aloud is to enjoy it. Let me say it again: your only job is to listen and feel the warm glow of words on a page. If those words attack you or reveal pain, you can show empathetic facial expressions and say words like, "Thank you for writing and reading that to me." In the next chapter, I'll give you lots of examples of how to respond to all sorts of freewrites.

✳ **Do not read your child's freewrite before you've heard it read.**

A caution to you, the grown-up: do not lay eyes on the freewrite before you've listened to the content. Why? Because your face may betray you! You'll scrunch your eyebrows when you see the sloppy handwriting or the poor spellings. Start with the content, always. Listen and be kind to the writer. Keep your face pleasant and curious. Smile or laugh or show kind concern if the topic is a difficult one. Be present.

There are lots of possible ways to continue a freewriting practice—including providing freewriting prompts. Once you get the hang of pure freewriting without a prompt, try using one to add a little spice and adventure to your writing time. The Brave Writer blog has Friday Freewriting prompts (for free!). You can also use any writing prompt you find online.

Here are a few ideas to get you started:

* Select the first line of a poem, copy it onto your own page, and then continue freewriting from there.

* Start each line with the words "If I could _____, I would . . ."

* Make a set of predictions for a year from now or ten years from now or one hundred years from now.

* Use any idiom as a prompt for freewriting. For example: When we say "Time flies," what do we mean?

If you've tried freewriting before and it fell flat or your kids didn't take to it, here are some troubleshooting tips:

* **Keep it private.**
Freewrite with your kids for four weeks without asking anyone to read their freewriting aloud. Let each person write whatever they want. You are not

to read any of their freewrites. Give each person a manila envelope that is only theirs to hold their writing. You may not look inside.

* **Keep it secret.**
Purchase a lock-and-key diary for each child. There's something about the protection of the lock and key that makes the writing itself feel like a secret, safe place to write.

* **Get off the table.**
Freewrite on clipboards. I have no idea why, but clipboards are magic for kids and allow them to choose other locations for writing besides the kitchen table. Freewrite on a picnic blanket, or lying on the floor, or up in a tree, or sitting on the trampoline, or at a coffee shop, or in a hidey-hole you make with sheets and a card table.

* **Change the writing tool.**
Bring a variety of writing implements to the table. Let everyone select which one they want to use. Try calligraphy and fountain pens, a handmade quill, felt-tip markers, pencils of various lead weights, roller ball pens, or anything else that strikes your fancy.

* **Change the writing surface.**
Try blank printer paper, graph paper, unlined paper, black paper with white gel pens, stationery, three-by-five note cards, small whiteboards, the walls

of your basement, sticky notes of various colors, cardboard, old paper grocery bags cut up, and so on.

* **Change how you use the paper.**
  Try turning the paper to landscape orientation, folding the paper into eight rectangular spaces to write in one space at a time, skipping lines, writing outside the margins, writing at an angle across a blank sheet of paper (so it's in a diamond shape), drawing a box and writing inside the box or around the edges, cutting a hole in a sheet of paper and writing around the hole, writing on a poster board hanging on the wall, or writing on paper hanging on an easel.

Freewriting liberates the writer to focus exclusively on their own thoughts without regard to the reader. It's a chance for the writer to fully inhabit their own experience of writing. It teaches a child *how to write*, often in a way that's invisible to you, the adult. Your kids will develop their own process that helps them become comfortable and competent writers.

WRITER REFLECTIONS

Most of us view a child's writing as flawed until someone "corrects" it. That correction might come from Grandma, who points out a misspelled word on the thank-you note your darling seven-year-old painstakingly wrote. It might come from your eyebrows furrowing as you read the sloppy handwriting of your third grader. It will definitely come from the child's

English teacher if this is a writing assignment that will be graded.

You know whose viewpoint is left out of all these assessments? The writer's! If we continue with the premise of this entire book—that writing is for the writer first and readers second—shouldn't we check in with the writer before offering any of our thoughts or suggestions? Wouldn't it be amazing to find out what this particular writing experience felt like *to the writer*?

Before we wade into the tricky territory of revision, let's start by giving our writers a chance to observe their process, comment on what worked and didn't, and listen to their thoughts about what they put on the page (or screen). I call this step in the process "Writer Reflections." By inviting your child to reflect on their freewriting experience, you help them name the tactics they used to generate what they wrote. You also allow them to let go of a difficult writing session because they will talk about it—learning what made it difficult.

Try one or two of these questions (be careful not to overdo it):

* How was today's freewriting session for you? Easy? Hard? Enjoyable? A struggle?

* What made it [easy, hard, enjoyable, a struggle]?

* When you felt stuck, how did you get unstuck?

* What was different about today's freewriting session compared with last time?

* What's your favorite sentence in today's freewrite? Why?

* Were you surprised by anything you wrote? What surprised you about it?

* When you finished, did you feel complete and satisfied, or is there more you wish you could say about this topic?

This is not a medical form in a doctor's office. These questions are open-ended and meant to spark a conversation, not complete a checklist. The idea is to help your child learn the power of self-observation. If you take notes or recall what your child says week to week, you can even use their own words to bolster them when they face a particularly challenging topic for writing. You might remind them of how they get "unstuck" or note what made one topic easy and another hard. Our kids live in the present. They aren't always as capable of recalling prior experiences to support themselves. By developing a "writer reflection" practice, you teach your children how to observe, know, and support themselves as writers.

Remember: for especially stuck and resistant writers, it's a good idea to freewrite weekly together for at least eight weeks before you revise *anything* your kids write. They get to throw away writing they don't like and experiment with different writing styles, but mostly they get to write without the fear that someone is going to tell them that they're doing it wrong. Once you've practiced freewriting together for at least eight weeks, you can enter a playful revision practice with them.

Your child will select one of their freewrites to use as a first draft. That draft will go through the revision process, and all the other freewrites will live forever as freewrites. The first type of revision practice we'll do together is exploratory and experimental; we'll save revising the paper in order to *improve* the writing for the following chapter.

PLAYFUL REVISION

Have you ever experienced this? Your child writes a draft of a paper. You're asked to read it to give comments. You notice the spelling and punctuation mistakes. You cringe at the lack of a transition or an abrupt conclusion. You pull yourself together and gently express these issues to your child. Instead of being grateful, your child wilts, cries, argues, or gets defensive. You explain that you were only trying to help and that you love the writing otherwise. Too late. Your child loses steam and now you have to drag that kicking and screaming writer across the finish line against their will. You wonder if it's even possible to work on writing without fits of anger or tears. You both dread the next assignment.

Revising original writing is one of the trickiest aspects of teaching kids to write. You're not alone in your frustration or worry. Revision can be a joy-filled, exploratory experience for the writer that doesn't lead to a meltdown. Truly! Unfortunately, most of us have no idea how to create those conditions.

Natural writers know that revision is the time when the writer gets to tinker with the words they've already put on a page. It's the moment when the exhausting first-draft energy abates and the playful, mess-with-it-six-ways-to-Tuesday energy emerges. Sometimes parents and teachers forget that before a child cleans up the mechanics, it's more important to enjoy having written. Moving words around, finding better ones, adding detail and research, making the writing pop—these are the enjoyable activities of the writer after freewriting and drafting. Think of revision like the step *after* you shop for furniture. Once the chairs, sofa, and coffee table are in the house, you move the furnishings around, add a throw pillow, brighten the room with paint, and put a few plants on stands to add warmth. Revision is that step—making the writing cozy and appealing.

In my work, I make a distinction between revising to *play around* with the writing and revising to *improve* the writing. In the former, which I'm covering in this chapter, the writer rewrites or reimagines the original draft in order to shake things loose and spark new ideas. In the latter, which I'll cover in the next chapter, the writer rewrites or reorganizes parts of the draft with an eye toward improving them. And both of these revision processes are separate from the editing process, in which the writer corrects the copy to match written English standards.

Can you imagine what might happen if you were to separate the task of revision from the task of correcting your child's spelling and punctuation when working with your child's writing? What if your child knew you weren't going to point out all their errors on the first read through, that you were instead interested in the content? Adults can help build the confidence of their young writers, or they can rattle them to the point where some kids never want to write again. As you recall from previous chapters, when we start by critiquing the mechanics, the child feels "unread." They lose motivation to work on the writing itself.

If you look back to the start of this chapter, notice that upon reading my short story, my mother didn't attack my lack of apostrophes. She jumped right into how the content impacted her. When she made suggestions, they felt like an investment in making my delightful writing even better! She invited me into a game and let me experience the difference the changes she had in mind would make.

Mistakes in grammar or spelling will keep. There's no need to fix them until the very end of the writing process (what I call the "mechanics mop-up" in the next chapter). Resist the urge to fix those mistakes and put your attention on the content first. Your kids will thank you—probably not audibly in actual words, but in their sweet little hearts where their fragile egos live.

LOW-STAKES REVISION STRATEGIES

The reason revision is so fraught is that most of us see revision as the requirement to *improve* the paper. The writer just excavated their insides to the best of their current abilities, yet the offering is seen as "not good enough yet." What a blow! Kids, especially, don't have enough experience with writing to see an adult's "kind" critique any other way. As a result, most revision experiences are "high stakes." High-stakes revision is about ensuring that the writer gets the writing *right*. But before a child can care about getting it right, they have to feel comfortable messing with that first burst of language. They have to know that behind the words they already put on the page are *more* words inside of them. Lots of kids don't know that this is true. They feel relieved to have gotten *any* words to the page, and now some adult is asking them for *more*?

To get comfortable with revision as a strategy for growing the writing, I prefer beginning with what I call "low-stakes" revision strategies. Kids can fiddle with their writing in ways that aren't intended to improve the writing at all. Rather, when using a low-stakes revision strategy, the child is growing their tolerance for altering the original. They're learning how to find additional words, ideas, or viewpoints for writing. They discover that it's not all that risky to move words around or to rearrange sentences into a new order. They stop seeing revision as an adult's opportunity to hurt their feelings.

Try these easy-to-use strategies at home without any pressure to perform for school. (For a comprehensive model, check out my Brave Writer curriculum called *Growing Brave Writers*, which includes even more methods for developing a robust revision strategy with students.) The practices I include here will help you and your child get started so that both of you are more comfortable with reimagining the original writing.

Strategy #1: Ruin the Original

Begin by giving your reluctant writers permission to do a little "violence" to the original. That word is startling, and it's meant to be. Let your child in on a secret: the first draft isn't permanent. The writer can mess with the first draft (or "ruin" it) without getting in trouble or causing sustained damage. To that end, keep the original freewrite separate from the copy you use for this revision step, so that the child knows that their freewrite is safely protected in case they want to go back to it. Breaking rules, changing the tone, flipping the viewpoint—

these practices can thaw a frozen writer. When you give your child permission to "ruin" the original, they feel empowered. They won't be subjected to an adult's scrutiny. They will knock the block tower over themselves and see what else can be built!

Sometimes writing *against* the original topic unearths new points of view. For example, if the prevailing perspective is that training a dog in obedience is necessary, your child might try writing about why obedience training wrecks a dog as a pet. Writing against the topic sometimes lets new ideas emerge that got overlooked in the original.

Another way to "ruin" the original is to change the format of the writing. For instance, turning a description into a poem might call up fresh language because the child is trying to find words that rhyme. If your child tells a story about the cat she loves, could she revise it to include the perspective of a person who finds the cat annoying? She might even try writing from the perspective of the cat! If a student writes about their best play in baseball, what happens if they flip it around to show the perspective of the other team as they watch that play being made? What if the student removes all the adjectives and only writes using verbs and nouns?

These kinds of approaches trick the mind of the student into playful thinking (rather than the tense, rigid mindset involved in making the freewrite more perfect for someone else). By following arbitrary rules or prompts, the child is provoked into creativity. Ruining the original is a delicious experience for many kids. It takes away the pressure to make the writing better, and ironically, sometimes this activity causes the writing and thinking to become clearer in spite of itself!

Here are a few other ways to "ruin" the original:

* If the freewrite is in third person ("he," "she," "they"), tell the story in first person ("I") or second person ("you").

* Change the main character of a story—from hero to villain, from a person to an inanimate object or animal, etc.

* Turn a narrative into a conversation only. If writing about a scientific discovery, for example, the child can write an interview with the scientist as though they were on a podcast or television show, imagining their replies.

* Turn a paragraph into a limerick or vice versa. What new language emerges? What new ways of saying the same ideas?

* Pick a fairly common letter of the alphabet, like *B*, *S*, *T*, or *C*. Make a list of words that relate to the topic and start with the same letter. Find places to put those words in the existing freewrite. Can your child make a sentence that includes several words that start with the same letter? How does that impact the writing?

* Roll a die. Use whatever number you roll in any one of these ways:
  - Add that number of facts.
  - Subtract that number of sentences.

- Count the words in the longest sentence. Shorten the sentence by the number you rolled.
- Count the words in the shortest sentence. Lengthen it by the number you rolled.
- Find that number of words to remove from the entire freewrite.
- Add that many words to the entire freewrite.

* Graph the freewrite.
  - Count the number of verbs, nouns, adjectives, and prepositions. What is the most common part of speech in this freewrite? Add a sentence using that part of speech.
  - Count the number of comparisons, facts, experiences, and descriptions. Which aspect of writing is most dominant in this freewrite? Add a sentence using one of the less dominant aspects of writing.
  - Count the number of letters used in each word. Find the average word length of this freewrite. Add two longer-than-average words and two shorter-than-average words.

* Print a fresh copy of the freewrite (triple spaced, large font). Hand a pair of scissors to your child. Ask them to remove (by clipping) as many words or sentences as they can while retaining the overall story of the freewrite. They can arrange those remaining words/sentences on a table, a cookie sheet, or the floor. They can put words back in if they need to in order to make sure it still makes sense.

* Deliberately rearrange the sentences. Using a pair of scissors, snip all the sentences into strips. Now reorder all the sentences so none of them follow logically. (This is harder than it seems but is a fabulous reverse psychology way of helping your kids experience and understand writing coherence.)

You'll think of other ways to ruin the original. The point is: when you say that revision starts with ruining the original, some children find that experience entirely liberating! The pressure is off. They can explore and experiment. There are also some kids who find this kind of revision a little terrifying. The ones who have been trained on the perfectionism model are especially nervous around the word "ruining." Instead, you might say, "I have some games for you to play with the original to see what else is hiding inside you!"

Try these low-stakes strategies for a while so that your child becomes comfortable *altering* the original. That's the goal here. Revision is the willingness to mess with the original, to change it in a meaningful way. In so doing, the child will often discover more powerful ways to express what they wanted to say in the original freewrite. If this happens, by all means let them modify the freewrite, adding to or subtracting from the original copy.

Strategy #2: Rewrite Notebook

One of the challenges of traditional high-stakes revision is that all the rewriting is happening on the page where that original draft lives. The additional marks and writing are an assault on that first effort, and some kids feel dispirited to see their hard work turned into a construction site. One writing mentor I admire told me she photocopies a student's writing and only writes her comments in pencil on the photocopy, in order to protect the original from that assault. That's a great tactic to use with kids who are especially sensitive. Another way to work with revision is to put your child in charge of the changes to be made. They can put their ideas in a "rewrite notebook."

Here's how it works:

1. Get a small notebook (kids love anything that fits their hands). Tell your child this is a place to keep track of small changes they might want to make to their current piece of writing. As they read their work, they can jot a note in the notebook to look at later.

2. Have your child read their draft or freewrite aloud. Encourage your child to notice what I call "label" words. These are terms that cover up the experience, like *awesome, great, ugly, stupid, fantastic, delicious, fun,* and *boring.* Most of these words end sentences. "Roller coasters are *awesome*" and "His birthday party was *boring*" and "I think all miniskirts are *ugly.*" These descriptive terms hide a wealth of experience just waiting to be excavated.

3. Jot down the sentence with the label word at the top of a unique page. (Do that for each sentence that contains a label word.)

4. Over a period of days, one at a time, chat with your child about these label-word sentences: *What was awesome about the roller coaster? The height, speed, the loop-de-loop?* Suggest your child pencil their answers into the notebook. They can be helped to conduct a little research. Put those notes into the notebook too. Don't try to cover all the label words in one day. Simply work through a word or two at a time over the course of a few days or a week.

5. Pick one of the label-word pages in the rewrite notebook. Set up a new freewriting time to explore that idea in more depth. If they like their additional ideas, they can then add that material to the original freewrite. Even if they don't add it, the exercise of digging a little deeper into the topic is a valuable process all by itself!

These two strategies for revision are not comprehensive. What they do is invite kids to experience what it feels like to bring their own critical thinking to their writing. Your kids determine what to change, what to notice, what to ponder further. They ask themselves what else they might say or think or feel about that topic. By introducing revision in this low-stakes way, you invite your child to build their stamina for higher-stakes revision practices that are intended to improve the writing, which we'll look at in the next chapter.

YOUR WRITING ASSIGNMENT

Use the freewriting and revision practices on your own this week. Try them out for yourself, away from your kids. You might want to head to the local library or a quiet coffee shop. Simply write. Play with revision. Get comfortable with these power tools for writing before you teach them to your kids. You'll be glad you did. Plus: now you have an excuse to head out the front door for a little "me time."

|||||||||||||||||||||||||

CHAPTER 9

Let Your Kids Clean Up Their Messy Writing

In the previous chapter, we talked about encouraging our kids to get messy with freewriting and playful revision practices. In this chapter, we'll talk about tidying up the mess with revision practices that improve the writing, followed by editing strategies that empower kids to correct their own errors in spelling, punctuation, and grammar.

But first, join me in my time travel machine. Let's go back to sixth grade. Can you recall your English teacher, your desk, the pale blue lines on the wide-ruled paper? Imagine, now, writing a three-paragraph report on a book you just read. You loved the book. You put your favorite words into these three paragraphs, like *cornucopia* and *outlandish*. You include some complex sentences that likely require commas and maybe even a semicolon, but you don't really know how to use those very well, so you guess. At the end, you're so pleased with yourself, you put a little joke—a punch line about the book—as a treat for your teacher, whom you adore.

When you finish, you hand it in. No one but the teacher is going to read this piece of writing: an audience of one. That teacher will return it to you at their convenience. Some diligent teachers turn around submitted writing in twenty-four to forty-eight hours, but most of them grade papers over the weekend (unpaid work for them, by the way). So it's not uncommon for that paper to be with your teacher for up to a week before you get it back. Once turned in, that paper usually vanishes from your awareness. Sometimes you forget you even wrote it by the time it's returned to you with a grade!

One day, the teacher arrives at class with a stack of three-paragraph papers. She distributes them to each student, usually silently. You look at the top page. Right near your name is a grade (sometimes the grade is at the end of the paper, but for a one-sheet, it's usually at the top). The location of the grade at the top right margin of the paper is convenient for the teacher, allowing them to flip through the stack and easily record the grades in their grade book. This location is inconvenient for you, however, because your seatmates may catch a glance of the grade you got. That grade tells a story—how the teacher felt about what you wrote.

Can you remember that feeling? I don't know any sixth graders who can look at that grade and say to themselves: "Even though I got marked down for not knowing how to use a semicolon, I trust that my teacher valued my thoughts." Instead, you likely assume that the grade represents the teacher's official, accurate reaction to your writing—how it felt to read your words and thoughts. Not only that, the grade is a message about how you stack up against other kids in your class as a writer. It's not just a message *to* you; it's a message *about* you and how you compare to other students your age.

As your eyes scan the paper, you notice red markings. (Today, some teachers use pencil or purple or green pens because they want their comments to feel less harsh—but, for reasons we're about to see, this doesn't actually soften the blow.) The markings show you which words you misspelled, what punctuation marks are incorrect or missing, and your mistakes in grammar. Occasionally, there's a comment about the writing itself. These comments range from "Nice!" to "Vague" or "Passive voice." A directive like "Don't put a joke in a report" might demoralize you when you were just trying to connect to the teacher with that punch line. Sometimes a comment will show you how to rework an awkward sentence or how to reorder a sequence of sentences to make a point clearer. Most comments are brief.

As you read, what are you thinking? What were you secretly hoping to read on that page from your teacher?

For most of us, we scan these comments a little defensively. We feel (justified or not) that we're being judged even though we did the best we could. The experience of a teacher's comments is not that we've been "read" but that we've been evaluated. To be corrected for a misspelling or punctuation error feels puzzling. If you don't know how to spell a word or you aren't confident in your use of a punctuation mark, why are you being held accountable for it? It's odd that we're marked down for what we don't yet know how to do reliably.

Many kids become a little desperate in that moment. Essentially, the grade tells them that they've *failed,* not that they're on a journey of mastery, one small step at a time. When kids believe that a teacher's comments will be punitive, they often dumb down their writing to match their skill level in spelling and punctuation. They give up the rich content they would offer if they were free to take that writing risk without fearing a penalty. Imagine that—we're training our kids to avoid complex sentences with sophisticated vocabulary just so that they can earn a break from criticism.

Back to your report with the red pen marks. Once you've finished reading what the teacher wrote in the margins, what do you do next? Do you make a note somewhere to remind yourself not to make those mistakes next time? Does the insertion of a comma in this one particular sentence make you any more knowledgeable about where to put a comma the next time? If a comment says "Vague," are you automatically able to make that sentence and future sentences clearer? If the teacher jots the note "Nice," can you be sure you understand what caught her attention in a happy way? Do you know how to produce that effect again?

Once a paper is finished and turned in, a student's interest in discovering how to improve their writing for that paper expires. The comments come too late—they're almost an afterthought. A writer is the most interested in improving their writing *while* they're still working on the paper. They need immediate, relevant, conversational feedback that they can apply right away. Delaying that feedback, sometimes for a week or more, means the student doesn't read teacher comments in order to grow as a writer. Rather, students merely want to know if they did a good enough job guessing what the teacher was hoping to find in their paper. They may hope to read a comment that tells them they did a good job, but that's not the same experience as having connected with a reader, which is the (sometimes secret) goal of anyone who writes anything.

When a teacher creates a writing assignment, an ideal version of what the writing will sound like and include springs to mind. This "ideal text" is hidden from the view of the students—and is often invisible to the teacher, too, since it's an automatic, often subconscious creation. Yet that ideal text is the metric by which student writing is measured. Kids understand this, even if they can't articulate it. When they go to write, they try to guess what kind of paper the teacher wants. They wonder about content, vocabulary, structure, and which point of view to take.

Frequently, students don't think about what *they* want to express or what the assignment calls to *their* minds. They're trying to mitigate the red pen remarks by guessing the teacher's ideal text and then writing *that*. The grade tells them how close they got. Here's what researchers have to say about the danger of the ideal text in classroom writing assignments.

> C. H. Knoblauch and Lil Brannon . . . pointed out [that] students produce assignments, not in order to be heard, but in order to give teachers something to judge on the basis of *their* [the teacher's] *agenda*. Since the teacher's agenda is usually the only one that matters, students have to puzzle out what the instructor wants—what in Knoblauch and Brannon's term constitutes the "Ideal Text."
>
> "To the extent that the teacher's expectations are not satisfied," they explain, "authority over the writing is stolen from the writer by means of comments, oral or written, that represent the teacher's agenda, whatever the writer's intentions may initially have been." That agenda distorts communication, when

teachers, who alone know what Ideal Text they have in mind, display little interest in understanding anything that differs from it.

Have you ever tried to hold a conversation with someone who has a hidden agenda? Have you felt the stress of guessing what the other person is thinking so you can avoid triggering their confrontational energy? That's a bit what it feels like when students go to write a paper for a teacher. When I first started teaching writing in the early 1990s, I ran across research into the significance of teacher comments on student writing. One of the staggering findings was that written remarks on student papers *didn't cause improvements on the next paper by the student.* In other words, those hours your teacher spent grading 125 papers over the weekend? Not a single margin note that the teacher painstakingly made resulted in better writing the next time around by any student. No impact whatsoever. That research floored me—but it makes sense when you learn that most teachers still do not receive training in their degree programs that teaches them *how* to offer this kind of responsive writing feedback to student writing.

You may be asking yourself what can be done about this conundrum. After all, your kids will have writing assignments and teachers for a good many years to come. Is there a better way to help students grow as writers while honoring the classroom agenda? As an important adult in a child's life, you have an amazing role you can play right now that will ensure your young writers keep growing in spite of any performance metric the schools use.

You get to be your child's first reader. As that reader, you can give your child the boost of satisfaction that comes from being read first and then supported in improving the writing. This writer-editor partnership is a sacred (and sometimes hilarious!) trust. You become a coconspirator in investigating your child's mind-life, sense of humor, amazing capacity to recall facts, and unique ability to create fresh comparisons. You get to point out tricks and tips that help make the writing pop to life. When a child feels read and admired, they want to figure out how to get that reaction again. You get to show them how!

If you catch on to this revision practice, you'll build a deeper relationship with your child as a by-product. They'll feel heard by you in a brand-new way. As their partner, coach, and ally, you'll help your kids develop into confident, competent writers in any environment.

REVISING TO IMPROVE THE WRITING

Freewriting and playful revision help your child become more and more comfortable with the writing process. They learn not to fear changing their first drafts and freewrites. They discover that more words do live inside them!

But there comes a time when your child will be ready to *improve* their writing—to enrich and enhance it. Writers call that process revision. Revision doesn't mean, however, hacking the original writing to bits with a red pen. The red pen suggests that there's something wrong with the original writing a child submits for grading, which we now know is not true; the marks on the page have value already, before we do anything else to them!

Instead of marking up your child's work (or giving it a bunch of cotton candy compliments), I suggest practicing what I call "reader response feedback." The basic premise is this: You're an enthusiastic, curious reader who *wants* to connect to the writing. You'll notice what works well and say so, and you'll make kind observations that motivate your child to improve the writing. With a friendly attitude and a few key strategies, you can turn the revision process into one that creates a closer relationship between the two of you—and better writing too!

Reader Response Feedback

"Reader Response Feedback" is a strategy I developed that puts the key goal of writing at the center of the revision process. Writers want readers to *read* them first for the content. They aren't interested in how to improve their writing until they feel read for what they've already offered. To provide this kind of response means that you read the writing first as a reader—noting all the ways the writing impacts you. Then, you respond by carefully choosing words that connect to your child's heart.

It's not a strategy for "correcting" the writing, though suggestions that help *grow* the writing are valuable. You strip yourself of the notion that you know what ought to be on the page (the ideal text in your imagination) and get interested in the writing your child offers. Your goal is to pay attention to how the writing strikes you, how it holds your attention or catches you off guard or offers you a perspective. You notice how the writing lands in your body—nervous stomach, tightened jaw, relaxed shoulders, a smile forming on your face, a quick intake of breath due to a surprise, laughter, warmth running through your core.

As you read and note these reactions, you give your child valuable feedback that helps them understand how they accomplished that impact. First, you may show them how they unwittingly used a literary device to achieve that pleasing effect on you. Second, you may be able to note places where they can dig a little deeper to expand the writing so that it adds clarity or emotion. A writer grows when they understand how they were successful and where they still fall a little short of the *desired impact*. Read that again. We want the comments we offer to support the writer in *their* goals for *their* writing. They aren't interested in comments that simply tell them they didn't live up to your expectations.

Let me say it another way—more directly.

After your child has written, they're usually not very curious about whether or not they left out a comma. That's not the first question they have when they hand over a piece of writing to a friend or parent or teacher to read. What they want to know is:

* Did you like it?

* Did you get it?

* Did you feel the feelings I was hoping to cause?

* Did you agree?

* Were you interested in my conclusion or ending?

* Did you notice my clever language or devastating logic?

      * Could you see in your mind's eye the image I tried
        to convey?

These are the kinds of questions a writer has, even if they
haven't voiced them. *They wonder if their writing is worth
reading.* If the first comment they hear back is "You left out a
comma," the writer assumes that the writing is so dull, the
only thing the reader noticed is a missing comma. None of
their flights of fancy or neatly paced points could overcome
poor punctuation. To create this healthy writer-editor partnership with your kids, you have to begin as a reader.

The following guidelines can help you offer kind, beneficial feedback for any kind of writing your child tosses your way!

Read the writing once without judgment.

Begin by letting your child know that it's your pleasure to read
their writing. Keep your face relaxed. Be led by curiosity about
what's on the page. Let go of the temptation to judge or grade
the paper, even invisibly in your mind. Your first task is simply
to *read* what's there and to be curious about it. We'll talk about
what to do with writing that tests you—the kind that feels like
it's an attack or that is meant to provoke you into criticism.
For now, let's start with garden-variety writing. Your child
freewrites, and you're going to read it first with an open, curious mind and a loving, unbothered expression on your face.

Read the writing a second time, noting your reactions as you read.

This is the key shift in how to give feedback to a writer. Read as a reader. On this read through, you'll focus on what works in the writing (all the ways the writing is effective in communicating with you as a reader). Think about each sentence and note what your body and mind do in reaction. Keep a record of your reactions. For instance, if the opening sentence grabs your attention, notice. Jot that down. If, two sentences further into the piece, the child offers a great description that creates an image in your mind, note that. Your child might write: *Kelly, my dog, has fur the color of charcoal.* Perhaps you felt a little warmth run through you and you instantly pictured Kelly, the dog, in your mind's eye. Make a note as though you're speaking to your child directly: "I can picture that dog in my mind! Charcoal is a great description that helps me see the color black." The goal is to note what's working already in the piece and to name it. You don't have to express elaborate comments to show that the writing impacted you. Your natural enthusiasm and caring tied to a specific comment are enough.

Perhaps you notice a powerful metaphor: *My Blow Pop has a ring around it like the planet Saturn.* You could write a note like this one: "That's a great comparison! You're using what's called a 'simile'—when you compare one item to another using the word 'like' or 'as.' How cool is that?" When your child demonstrates mastery of the facts in a particular arena, you might feel a surge of pride. Count how many facts your child included about World War II tanks and give them a total. You might say, "By the time I got to the end of this paragraph, I had read six facts that increased my understanding of tanks. For instance, I had no idea that a tank could do [X] or that a tank weighs [Y]. Truly amazing!" When you read as a reader, you give your child the insights they need into how and why they're already communicative writers.

Let's look at two journal entries my daughter Johannah wrote at age nine. Our family moved from California to Ohio. She kept a diary to process her feelings of grief. The first entry is about leaving California, and the second one was written after we arrived in Ohio. For the sake of this chapter, I'm writing the kinds of comments I would give to this writing. Notice her spelling and punctuation errors, yes. But use this chance to practice ignoring them and managing your facial expressions. Lean in to the narrative the way she crafted it. Pay attention to how she involves you in her emotions through the imagery. My responses are in italics.

It's wet and cold outside. Today is the last time I'm going to see Amanda for a long time. In movie's when someone is sad, it's raining.

Ah, Johannah, I'm going to miss Amanda too. I like how the rain matches your mood. I am right here with you in your sadness.

I never realized that it happens in reel life too.

So insightful to notice this! That must be why they use rain for sad moments in the movies, because sometimes life is like that too. Rain reminds me of tears.

The grass is wet but not Shinning there's no light.

The lack of light and the fact that the wetness is not shining match the mood you're creating. I feel sad and dark reading it.

Our car is sopping wet. Little wet yellow flowers shine like Gold in the misty darkness.

So poetic! Right when I feel the saddest, you offer me hope in the form of a little shining flower. Genius! You're able to see some beauty in spite of everything. I felt relief when I read the idea that even in the dark, there is still beauty to notice.

I'm going to miss Amanda a lot. The little pink spring flowers are getting weter bye the second, It's so close to moving day it's so hard to believe I'm moving. I can't stop crying. It's hard to say goodbye to friends, very good friends. These are tears. [She drew some tears here.]

It is hard to say goodbye to friends. When you say it twice in a row, emphasizing that Amanda is a very good friend, I feel the loss even more keenly. I see your tears. I have some too.

[My daughter continued this entry on another day, after we arrived in Ohio.]

It just stopped raining. Everything that is green is shining like dimons in the ruff.

I love how you have incorporated this saying from the movie Aladdin! *You also hint at hope in this new place, which feels reassuring.*

The trees are bare there's not one leaf on them. You can hear the whistling of the birds but you can't see them.

These two sentences use imagery to convey feelings— what you can't see, what's missing—just like your friend Amanda.

The sky is white and a little bit blue but I don't understand why people call it gray because it is definitely not gray.

Excellent detailed observation that surprised me. Now I'm wondering if the sky is ever actually gray. I want to go outside to look! It's a good question too. I wonder what we mean by gray sky.

The wind is shaking the freezing green grass.

Personification! The wind is doing the shaking—like a person might. I can see that in my mind.

Johannah, I loved these two journal entries. You created a mood through your careful observation of the weather and nature. You used imagery (wet, not shining, gold in the misty darkness, little pink spring flowers, green diamonds in the rough, bare trees, whistling birds, sky that's a bit blue, freezing green grass) to take me on the journey of your feelings about moving. By the end I feel both your sadness and a tiny sliver of hope for a better future. Thank you for sharing that with me.

Notice that these comments are entirely positive. I chose to ignore anything that didn't work. In the early phase of building trust with your young writers, your reader response feedback task is to focus on how the writing moved you or surprised you or gave you chills or made you proud. By highlighting what's effective about your child's writing, you reinforce those choices. When you name the literary device behind that choice, your student learns that they're writing with skill, not just hitting a random moment of writing power. Your kids can then mentally populate their writing tool kits with their best strategies. They can use those techniques again and again. You might even say on a future paper: "Remember how powerful it was to include facts in your description of tanks? Let's go get some facts for this topic."

Let's look at a freewrite by a nine-year-old Brave Writer student (let's call him Max) that is more focused on facts than imagery. My comments to him about his writing follow in italics.

I like fish

I'm eager to read more about what makes you like fish!

They come in all collers and shapes and sizes

I immediately started picturing the fish I've seen. I wonder what colors and shapes and sizes are in your mind when you write this!

But I think what I like most about fish is that they live and breath in the oacean,

That's an amazing truth about fish that we so often forget. Thanks for reminding me to appreciate that fact!

The ocean it is so wet and cold and dark and mysterious with so many fish and sharks

These words create body sensations for me—wet, cold, dark, and mysterious. The ocean where the fish live is so different from the ocean I enjoy when on the beach. I felt curious and noticed a little tingle on my spine too.

I like sharks. They can smell a drop of blood in 3,000 gal of water.

Okay, now I'm nervous! One drop of blood in 3,000 gallons of water is so tiny! That's an impressive fact to include.

One looks like a 2 sided hammer the other looks like a monster with a huge mouth and teeth as long as my hand

Excellent images! A two-sided hammer is exactly what a hammerhead shark looks like, and the idea that a shark's tooth could be as long as your hand really clarifies the size of those huge teeth! This is a terrific, fact-filled freewrite about fish and sharks!

Over the last twenty-five years of teaching writing at Brave Writer, one of the interesting discoveries we've made is that if we write our comments beneath chunks of student text as we read along, the student *feels* read. They can see the journey our minds went on when we read their writing. Though I stumbled on this format over email back in the early 2000s, we continue to use it in our online classes today. Why? Because putting our feedback in writing that addresses each part of the paper helps the student experience us as *partners* in the writing process rather than *evaluators*. What we've found out from decades of this kind of reader response feedback is that when kids feel respected and read, and the comments we share have meaning, they grow as writers. In fact, they care about improving their writing.

You, as the important adult in your child's life, can do something similar. You can take the paper that your child has written and type it into a Word doc (retaining the punctuation and spelling mistakes). You can then triple space and type your comments under each chunk of writing, printing it all at the end. Another way to offer this style of written feedback is to photocopy the original, clip it into chunks, and glue these to a sheet of paper, handwriting your comments between each chunk. Keep the original clean, but create a photocopy for commenting.

As I was working on this book, a mother sent me a delightful example of how this reader response feedback model became powerful in their family. The daughter, Natalie (age eight), took one of our writing classes with her mother. The instructor, Kim Misra, used this style of feedback for Natalie's writing. Natalie was so impressed by that experience, she turned around and gave writing feedback to her little brother, Dave (age five), in the spirit of Mrs. Misra's comments. Here's the email she sent her teacher, proud of her work as a reader of her brother's writing. She included some of the ways we invite *more* writing, too, which you'll see in the next part of this chapter.

Dear Mrs. Misra,

I really enjoyed your Brave Writer 101. My brother Dave (5) wrote a freewrite and I gave feedback like you do! I'm excited to be a writing coach. Here is his freewrite and my feedback!

— He is cute, he is snuggly.
— *Who is he? Dave, your start has me hooked.*
— Well, I'd say he is fluffy.
— *How fluffy? You could do some revision and describe how fluffy it is.*
— We snuggle him a lot. His feet are gigantic, they are bigger than my head.
— *Wow! Maybe you could measure his feet to give your readers an idea of how big they are.*
— He is Papa Bear!
— *Wow! I love how you wait to tell me who "He" is!*
— He hugs us. He has very fluffy hugs. His hands are almost as big as my head. He is a stuffed animal bear, either a short face or brown bear.
— *Wow again! I love how you leave me with a kind of a question to think about.*

Signed,
Natalie (8) feedback in the style of Brave Writer Coach

I can't stop smiling! This is so cute. I especially love the way she says "Wow!" over and over again. When you really read a child's writing, you can't stop yourself from exclamations of delight.

Once you've taken notes throughout the read through, you can share them with your child orally or in writing. Some kids like having a conversation. Some like reading your remarks so they can process them alone, without you present. Both work. If this is your first time giving feedback, focus exclusively on positive comments that demonstrate that you've read the writing, you like what they offered, and you can see the writing techniques they used effectively. No need to point out items for improvement in the first few reader response sessions. By the way, it's fine if you only find two or three items for comment.

Make sure your feedback is specific.
With reader response feedback, you aren't just giving compliments, like "Nice" or "Good job" or "I loved it!" Rather, you're skillfully naming why a child's writing already has elements in it that work.

Here are tips to support this practice.

* **Notice what works as you read the writing.** Pay attention to how the writing lands with you. Be on the lookout for quality language, good imagery, details, integration of facts, sequence of ideas, and how the writing engages your imagination.

* **Identify how a particular writing choice impacted you.** Did you feel an emotion? Are you better

informed? Did you have an unexpected moment of delight? Were you surprised by a fresh comparison? Did you notice a novel vocabulary word? Say so, specifically.

* **Name the writing technique.** Did your child use a simile or make an analogy? Were the words inadvertently alliterative (a few words start with the same sounds)? Did your child sequence a series of steps clearly or include dialogue that was believable or list a set of facts that were relevant and interesting? Notice and name.

There are loads of literary techniques we all use naturally and some that we learn and explore in writing. Your task is to highlight to the best of your ability the tactics that work for you, as a reader. You may not know all the names of those devices. That's okay! Simply offer your reaction with as much genuine warmth and specificity about *how* the writing landed with you as you can. For instance, your child might write: *Thatcher had the last laugh.* You may not know that the repetition of the internal vowel sound is called "assonance," but you could comment that you enjoyed reading those words in a row and hearing them in your mind because of that repeating /a/ sound. This is the kind of comment from an adult that feels so good to hear as a child writer. It's these specific sorts of remarks that let your child know you read them well.

Here are some of my favorite writing techniques to notice in a child's writing.

* **Surprise**

  The element of surprise is perhaps the most important literary device—and rarely taught. Sometimes your child will give you a surprising, apt description that invites you to see the image, situation, story, or character more clearly. An opening hook, a unique vocabulary word, a fresh comparison, a startling fact, an unexpected twist—any of these will cause the reader to *keep reading.*

* **Humor**

  Never underestimate the power of humor in writing! One of my twelve-year-old students wrote about the trebuchet (a kind of weapon from the Middle Ages that hurls rocks over city walls). When he described it, he used humor to help the reader grasp what it does: "I would like to have [a trebuchet] in my backyard and then I could crush the people I didn't like with my brothers who I would shoot out of the trebuchet." Clearly he was having fun, but you can also feel the power of the description too!

* **Literary devices that play with sound**
  These include:
  - **Alliteration:** Repeated initial consonant sounds in multiple words (good as gold, follow your feelings)
  - **Assonance:** Repeated internal vowel sounds in multiple words (between trees, the light shines bright)

- **Consonance:** Repeated consonant sounds inside multiple words (pitter patter, Lucky Strike)
- **Onomatopoeia:** Words that express the sound they represent (cock-a-doodle-do, zing, bam, snort)
- **Rhyme:** Words that share similar-sounding endings (dream and scream, through and flew)

* **Skillful use of syntax**
  This could include:
  - **Vivid verbs:** Action verbs, particularly those that transform a noun into a verb, like "She hopscotched to the mailbox." Another sort of vivid verb is one that borrows a verb from one context and applies it in a new context, like "The moonlight sliced the tree in two." ("Sliced" is a vocabulary word associated with cooking yet is used here in an active, metaphorical way to talk about moonlight.)
  - **Specific nouns and adjectives:** "Amish hickory rocker" rather than "chair," or "black-capped chickadee" rather than "bird."
  - **Fresh descriptions:** Instead of "the scary ride," the novelty of "the stomach-churning ride."

* **Comparisons that work**
  Some examples:
  - **Metaphor:** A comparison in which one thing is said to *be* another: "The tree was a broomstick," or "Her hair is a bird's nest."

- **Simile:** A comparison in which one thing is said to be *like* or *as* another: "The tree is like an upside-down broomstick," or "Her hair was as tangled as a bird's nest."

* **Setting and mood**

The setting creates a mood. Some kids are naturally skilled at creating an experience for the reader—drawing in details from nature, lighting, weather, seasons, and more. If you notice that you feel dark and gloomy or bright and happy as you read, see if you can trace it back to word choices that indicate the setting or mood. Here's a sample from a female student, age eight: "I woke up to the sun rising. Have you ever seen it rise? I felt the warmth through my fingers, and all through my body. I felt as if I was the sun, always gold and warm, never cold. I felt as if I was the most contented person on earth."

* **Facts and figures**

Notice when your child weaves in the facts they know, when they use any numbers in their descriptions, when they cite an expert's opinion, or when they give detailed steps in sequence. These are high-level expository writing skills. Here's an example of specific numbers showing up in a nine-year-old student's writing: "The Rapid Fire Nerf gun comes with twenty darts. The extra darts come in packs of ten. You pump the gun thirty times to shoot the darts."

* **Fluent, natural language**

Look for those aspects of the writing that sound like your child and are easy to read and understand. Affirm those sentences! Kids are too often dinged for vague prose. You have the chance to isolate the parts of the writing that are easy to understand and that signify the unique style of your child. Here's a sample from my daughter Johannah, age nine, that sounded just like her: "When I look at my mom's guitar, I think, 'Let me at it!' The neck is heavy and sturdy like a tree branch. The body is hollow and light. There's a big cave in the body where the music comes out. The first two strings feel soft like thread. The wood of the guitar smells like a forest. The edges are pale yellow like a melon that's not ripened. I pick up my mom's guitar and I strum it. Its music is soft like a feather against my neck."

What if there's nothing to compliment?

In some cases, your kids are so stuck, they will test you to see if you meant it when you said "Write whatever comes to mind." That's the moment when you need to dig deep and commit to this process of being a *reader*—not a parent or teacher. They may hand you a freewrite like this one from a thirteen-year-old boy:

I have Writer's Block. Why do I have Writer's Block? I don't know. How long have I had Writer's Block? I don't know. I can't stop having Writer's Block. [He went on like this for several more sentences.]

You may wonder: *How on earth can I give feedback to a piece of writing that says nothing of value?*

The answer is: Any writing a child offers has value. All of it counts. Think about the babbling your baby did before they uttered recognizable speech. This kind of freewriting is babble— it's hooking up the hand with the mind and allowing the hand to take dictation. In this freewrite, the child is telling you the truth—they are struggling with writer's block (whatever that means to the child). Look at how he takes pains to express it in writing anyway! That's worth noting all by itself. For a truly blocked and reluctant writer, I would start with a simple statement of thanks. "Thank you for writing."

Or you might try one of these:

* "Thank you for writing the whole time."

* "Thank you for writing your real thoughts."

* "It must be hard to have writer's block, and yet you wrote anyway. Thank you."

For some kids, asking a follow-up question is a gentle way to show support through curiosity. You might ask, "When you use the term 'writer's block,' I'm curious what that means to you. What would it be like not to have writer's block anymore? What would you write about if you didn't have writer's block?"

When you take the content seriously, you show your child that they can trust you with more writing. As a reader, you're acknowledging that the writer took a risk to put the truth of their thoughts and feelings into words on a page. That's a vulnerable act, and it deserves to be held with love. Sometimes that simple acceptance makes space for the child to write something else next time. One student of mine, Logan, age ten, wrote how much he hated writing on day one of his free-writing experience. By day three, he had composed a paragraph about his fantasy of going on a camping trip to look for bears with his dog and his dad. When a child tells you that they hate writing or that they're struggling to think of words to write, they're really asking, "Can the real me show up here? Will I get in trouble if I say what I'm really thinking?" It's our job to say: "It's *all* welcome."

What about those kids who write the word *poop* sixteen times? Same thing. You might say: "Thanks for writing the whole time." Or if you feel spunky and your relationship allows it, you might say back playfully: "That's a lot of poop!" Then move on with your day. After a while, trying to shock your parent gets boring. Eventually most kids settle into writing about something else. These attempts to jar you or to tell you their truth (even "I hate this. I hate school. I hate writing. I hate you") count as writing! If the goal is teaching your kids to write, honoring their risky self-expression is the first step toward unlocking your struggling writer.

Once you've established a good connection with your child, and your child has written a draft of material that would benefit from a revision process that *improves* the writing, you can move to the suggested practices that follow in this chapter.

Narrow the Focus, Expand the Writing

Only adopt this practice *after* you've provided positive reader response feedback first on multiple unrevised freewrites. Ask your child to select a freewrite for the revision process (hopefully they have six or eight freewrites and choose one of them). Begin by identifying the places in the writing that need amplification—the parts of the writing that are vague, weakly phrased, or not as strong and clear as they could be. This is what I call the "narrow and expand" part of the reader's response. The reader narrows their focus to one item (a single word, a missing step, a brief description, the absence of facts). Then the reader asks the writer for "more." Rather than suggesting that the writer hasn't done a good enough job yet, the reader zeroes in on an aspect of the writing that would benefit from *more writing*. **Narrow the focus, expand the writing.** Each item is addressed one at a time.

When we ask for "more writing," we're saying that we have faith that the additional details or descriptions or facts are within reach of the young writer. This act of faith is a different experience than critique. Rather than saying, "You should have included more facts, so I'm marking you down," you're saying, "I see where you're going. Let's add more writing to enrich what you've already written." Can you feel the subtle difference here?

As the reader, you will offer suggestions as questions and options, not critiques or judgments. You won't say: "There aren't enough facts in this paragraph." You will say: "I'd like to know *more* about tanks. What do they weigh? How fast can they travel? What are they made of?"

If you want more descriptive detail, you won't say: "Add better descriptive terms." You will say: "I'd love to read *more* detail about this scene. I want to see what you see. Can you paint a picture for me? What's in the sky? What color are the flowers? What's the weather like?"

If you want a child to dig deeper into an experience, you

won't say: "This section is vague." You will say: "In this paragraph, you describe feeling uneasy before the piano recital. Tell me *more* about 'uneasy.' What was going on in your body? Where did you feel your nerves? What racing thoughts were you having, if any?"

If you want your child to add dialogue to a scene, you won't say: "You need dialogue here."

You'll say: "I would love to hear these two characters talk to each other. Can you give me *more* conversation between them about . . . ?"

The goal is to treat the existing writing as a map to *more* writing. Avoid telling your child that they've failed to live up to a standard or that they were wrong to write in the way that they did. Instead, ignore blatant mistakes or sentences that don't work. Focus on the places where a child's writing can be expanded.

Here are a few more types of comments you can make in this phase of reader response feedback:

* I want to see the beach the way you see it. Pretend you're making a movie. Put the camera lens on the ocean: What do you see? What do you hear? What's in the sky? How big are the waves? Now move the lens to the wet sand. What color is it? Is anyone digging into the sand? Are there sand crabs? Now move the lens to the dry sand. What do you see on the shoreline? What do you hear or smell? What activities are happening? Who's at the beach?

* I can tell that you love brushing your horse every day from this sentence. Can you help me, the reader,

understand why daily brushing matters? Let's put that right here.

* I was eagerly following you in that description of level two of your video game. Then I got a little lost! I know you're the expert and I'm still learning. Can you fill in this missing piece for me?

* I loved this sentence! It surprised me and gave me chills. I wonder what would happen if we moved it to the (beginning, end) of this story. Want to test it to see?

These sorts of comments come from love. You love your kid, you love their self-expression, you want more of who they are and what they know in their writing. Your posture is not condescending, it's not punitive or corrective, it's not overly enthusiastic (and sometimes phony) cheerleading. It's realistic, accurate feedback, based on reading the writing as a reader who wants to get the most out of what the child cares to communicate.

We can always offer our children support for whatever writing they produce, even when they're deliberately trying to thwart the writing process or to push us away. Here's a beautiful freewrite by a twelve-year-old describing this exact experience.

One day my mom tells me I need to do some freewriting. On this day I am committed to not doing it, so I come up with an amazing and devious plan to avoid having to write more. I take my pen in my hand, and I wait for my mom to set the timer, and I start writing. Except I use a bunch of abbreviations. I wrote down "lil" instead of "little" and I didn't use any punctuation or capital letters, and I just wrote about video games. I was hoping that my mom would be annoyed enough with me being so bad at writing that she wouldn't ask me to write anymore. But instead, she just told me I did a really good job and that she liked what I said about my video games. It was nice. My mom is nice.

After you've thoroughly honored the original piece of writing, pick two or three items to expand on. When you identify a sentence or a part of the freewrite that needs expansion, your child will narrow their focus to that one item and freewrite about it on a separate sheet of paper (or a new document on the computer). You can use the freewriting guidelines in chapter 8. Once your child has written more, those sentences can be integrated into the original freewrite. You can look at them together and even create sentences to hook the new material to the existing draft.

By the way: This is *exactly* how professional writers work. They get the raw copy going, and then they come back and work on bits and pieces a little at a time. They narrow their focus to that one idea that needs development or the place where they left out the research because they were too busy writing the draft. With a fresh start and more time, they return and make the existing draft more precise. They hunker down with one detail or one weak paragraph and give their full, revitalized energy to that part of the writing. They write *more*. They toss in a transition or two and incorporate the new writing into the existing draft. Kids don't know that they're allowed to do this until someone shows them the way. That can be you!

Be careful not to overdo it in this stage of development. Most kids can handle making a couple of improvements per paper. Then they're tapped out. Remember: *writing growth happens over a series of writing projects over a period of years.* You do not have to make each paper perfect or publication-worthy. Whatever issue you don't work on in this paper is bound to reappear in a future one, and you can work on it then. It may be that once you work through the two to three items for narrowing and expanding the writing, your child is done. Wonderful!

EDITING: PUT THE RED PEN IN YOUR KID'S HAND

Once you have a finished draft, it's time to polish it! After revision comes editing. Editing—or copyediting, if you want to get technical—is the process of correcting grammar, spelling, and punctuation errors. You won't be making these corrections yourself, by the way. It's your child's turn to edit their own paper. That's right! They can do it. Let me show you how.

I call this part of the process the "mechanics mop-up." Here's what's amazing. Once your child has thoroughly worked with the content—moving bits of writing around, changing the language, and adding details or facts—they'll be ready to correct any spelling or punctuation mistakes without much fanfare. Lots of kids love this part of the process, and you're about to see why. They feel well read and that the ideas on the page are worthwhile. Now, they get to wield the red pen to tidy it up! They experience the power of bringing order to their final draft.

Your child will be the one to go through their own paper and identify any missing punctuation, misspellings, and awkward phrasing that they can detect. Your child doesn't need to know if *you* know how to spell and punctuate. They need to find out if *they* know. By putting a little time and distance between the revision process and the editing process, you let your kids approach the writing with a completely different mindset. They'll read their writing like a third-party reader. They'll notice mistakes they made in the draft that eluded them when they were deep in the weeds of generating language. You'll be amazed at their ability to spot mistakes in their own writing when they're empowered to be the ones to go find those mistakes. Give them an editor's visor and their favorite red pen! Turn them loose!

The Mechanics Mop-Up Model

Follow these steps in the mechanics mop-up model for the best outcomes and biggest growth opportunity.

1. Ask yourself: What elements of standard written English can my child reliably implement correctly? Periods? Capital letters at the beginning of sentences and in proper nouns? What tricky spelling word (like *because*) is my child learning right now? What would be worth double-checking, like using *they're*, *their*, and *there* appropriately? Make a list. Consult your child too. If they tell you, "Yes, I know periods well, but I'm bad at commas," leave commas off the list.

2. Select the three to four items you both feel confident your child can double-check and correct.

3. Create a note card and put those items on it.

4. Hand that note card to your child and say these exact words: "Hey, (insert name). It's time to edit your draft. *Make sure you like all of your spelling, punctuation, and grammar choices.*" Notice my language here. We aren't asking a child to fix mistakes. We're asking the child to make editorial decisions—to make sure that the paper is as close to what the child wants it to be as possible. That means considering a spelling or evaluating the absence of a punctuation mark. By calling it a "choice," you let your child operate with authority. This creates a feeling of power in writing.

5. Next, say this: "Here's a note card with a few grammar, spelling, and punctuation items that you know well. Use this guide to help you look at each item in your draft to make sure you like the choice you made. If you don't, you can make the change right on the page. Feel free to make other changes to spelling and punctuation that aren't on the note card if you notice them as well."

6. Once your child has gone through the paper using the note card as a guide, they're finished. Anything your child "missed" is something that child does

not yet know! No need to hold them accountable for what they haven't mastered. Make a note of those spellings or missing punctuation marks and then work on those skills in the coming weeks, outside of original writing and school. (See chapter 11 for ideas about how to do that.)

7. If this is a paper that is meant to be read by anyone who would criticize your child's writing, like Grandma, your next step as the adult is to clean up the remaining errors without discussion or fanfare. That means *you* will fix the errors yourself. Protect your child from random grammar attacks. If the paper is for a school assignment, you can leave in the remaining mistakes, since that's an accurate reflection of your child's current skills. The important thing to say to your child, though, is this: "Your paper is ready to turn in. It's fine with me if your teacher corrects any remaining mistakes, because you and I both know you don't have those skills down pat yet. You're still learning. We'll keep working on them together."

A good habit to teach your children is to get a second set of eyes on any piece of writing before they "hand it in," whether it be to a teacher at school or to an editor at a publishing house. While your child lives with you, you get to be that second set of eyes. Your kids will trust you to be gentle and dispassionate— to help them mop up their mechanics, not to judge them for "making the same mistake again." When your students go off to college, they can ask a roommate or go to the writing lab to get that second pair of eyes on their papers before they turn them in. When we try to proofread our own work, our familiarity with the paper makes it difficult to catch typos that somehow sneak through the editing process. (This is true even for professional copyeditors and proofreaders!)

Taking responsibility for the well-edited, final paper is the character quality you want to develop in your child. Your kids will use spell check and grammar check—as they should. They can ask you to do a final read through after they've made as many edits as they can. Remember: it takes about ten years to gain fluency in writing, so your expectations for an eight-year-old should not be the same as your expectations for an eighteen-year-old—which we'll discuss in the next chapter.

YOUR WRITING ASSIGNMENT

When using the techniques discussed in this chapter, how did it feel to read as a reader rather than someone critiquing your child's writing? What adjustments did you have to make in order to focus on the content before you provided copyedits? Did you train yourself to smile? Did you find yourself earnestly looking for what to compliment? How was that experience for you? How was it for your child? Journal your thoughts.

||||||||||||||||||||||

CHAPTER 10

How Writers Grow Naturally

He's doing it! Look! Timothy let go of my hand—he's walking!" My friend Laura collapsed in relief, as if she had just gotten her tax refund after thinking it was lost in the mail. She'd been agonizing over the fact that my son Noah, three months younger, had been walking for two whole days already. She'd suffered an eternity of worry in those harrowing forty-eight hours.

Laura celebrated momentarily, then flipped around to ask my opinion: "Do you think I can say Tim walked at twelve months since he doesn't turn thirteen months old until tomorrow?"

I blinked. Was she serious? How could she care about something so trivial? But the fact was, parenting books told her most kids learn to walk by their first birthday. She wanted her kid to be *normal*—to be like "most" kids. It was a blow to think Timothy hadn't lived up to that standard. But no matter how much Laura wanted her son to be the poster child for growing and developing at the so-called appropriate rate, Timothy walked when he was ready. No medical chart or comparison to another kid sped him up.

It's tempting to let someone tell you what to expect of your kids. A whole industry's worth of parenting books have titles that start with *"What to Expect When . . ."* Every parent wants reassurance that their child is progressing at the right rate, doing the right things. At what age should they be weaned from the bottle or breast? When can they ride a two-wheeled bike alone? How can you know your child is ready to bathe without supervision? No matter what the books or websites tell you is the common age for a typical child to do those tasks, you're stuck with the kids you actually have—the ones who never align perfectly with the suggested timeline.

In writing, we face the exact same situation. Curriculum developers and school boards put together what they call a "scope and sequence" for each grade level and subject area— essentially, a "what to expect when" model that describes the particular skills a child ought to learn at each age, and in which order those skills should be taught. (You can search online to see the scope and sequence your local school uses for each grade and subject.) When moving a large number of students through a curriculum, having a clear idea of what students ought to learn in a year is important. It also matters that what kids are being taught is appropriate for their stage of development. The scope and sequence provides this structure to educators.

That said, there's no official set of standards that represents the perfect guide to learning for all students. The scope and sequence for any subject is adjusted regularly to adapt to the most current research in education, but it doesn't adapt to the individual learner. If you have a child who takes a bit longer to learn to read than the typical first grader, you may worry that your child is "getting behind." A child can only "get behind" if someone has defined what the right pace of learning to read should be for everyone. Like my friend Laura, we're all subject to worrying that our child is not the typical student. That feeling of pressure can do damage to our kids. They may introject the feeling of not being smart enough, which then impacts their motivation to keep working at the challenging skill. Some kids then declare "I hate [fill in the subject]" as a way to avoid feeling bad about themselves.

In my work, I wanted to give parents a different kind of model to support growth in writing skills; to simply say a third grader should be able to write a report does nothing for the parent of a child who refuses to write or complains that their hand hurts after eking out three sentences. Instead, I got interested in how kids go from not writing at all to writing a little to writing well, regardless of age and writing format. I observed children from all walks of life and educational models. I thought back to my own childhood and how my writing journey evolved. I read research about the writing life—how it gets activated and cultivated. I read about what to do when a writer gets stuck, as all writers inevitably do. I taught my five unique children, who grew their skills at different rates. I put my tentative ideas into a guideline to help parents notice all the ways their kids are growing as writers right before their eyes.

I discovered that kids go through predictable patterns as they become independent writers. I've grouped my observations into five categories for ease of sorting. I've included some loosely defined age ranges for each one, but please please

please promise me that you'll disregard them if your child doesn't fit. I've seen sixteen-year-olds start in the first level (Jot It Down) and make it to the fifth level (Rhetorical Imagination) in two years. The older your child is, the easier it will be for that child to move through the natural stages of growth in writing, because they'll be more skilled hand writers, typists, and readers. Simply match your child to the stage of growth that corresponds to their current *writing* behavior and apply the principles and practices of that stage. No need to rush ahead to the "right" age. In fact, your child can't do the work of the later stage if they haven't developed the habits and skills of prior stages.

The goal is to move through these stages of growth in order. Each phase can come naturally if you know what to look for, support that development, and don't inadvertently expect a child to either skip a stage or to go through it alone (just like you wouldn't expect a child to ride a bike before learning to walk). Sometimes you'll revert to using strategies from a previous stage of growth to support a new writing demand at a more advanced level. Sometimes your child will startle you with their personal initiative in writing and leap forward. But by and large, these phases occur naturally when the adults in a child's life are relaxed, partner with their children, and have reasonable expectations. The bottom line is that modeling and encouragement are the most helpful tools for any writing program.

Use this set of descriptions as a quick recap for how to behave as the invested adult in your child's life and for clues that help you judge where your child is on the "journey to fluent writing" timeline.

JOT IT DOWN: BEGINNING WRITERS (0–7)

The first stage of growth is what I call the Jot It Down phase of writing. As we discussed in chapter 3, kids rely on you to be their secretary before they can write their own thoughts on the page. This is the stage of development that teaches children that their thoughts are worthy of being recorded in writing. There are lots of ways to explore writing when you act as your child's secretary. As children see their words filling up pages and booklets, they develop an appetite for writing—for the self-expression that becomes the basis for the writing they do themselves.

You can help your kids whet their appetites for the hard work of learning to read, handwrite, and spell by putting their thoughts into writing now. During the early years, be sure to introduce a phonics and handwriting program as well. Once your child is reading and handwriting easily, they are ready to move into the next stage of growth; if your child is not quite reading fluently at age eight, or if they have a learning challenge like dysgraphia or dyslexia, you may choose to stay in the Jot It Down stage of growth a little longer.

The Jot It Down strategy (being your child's secretary while they speak) is also a powerful tool for breaking through writer's block when a student of any age is struggling to find their words about a given writing topic. Sometimes just listening and scribbling the first few sentences or a set of ideas your older child shares with you gives that student the raw material to get started. (In chapter 12, we'll take a look at how an older student might use ChatGPT to get over that hurdle of starting from scratch as well.)

Your child may be in the Jot It Down stage of growth if they have several of these characteristics:

* Learning to speak

* Learning to read

* Learning to handwrite

* Eager to express themselves

* Makes marks on surfaces of all kinds

* Enjoys hearing you read aloud

* Loves the library

* Shows resistance to writing from scratch

* Declares, "I hate writing!"

* Finds a new writing format daunting

Writing Activities for the Jot It Down Stage

* **Booklet Stories**
  Fold sheets of paper in half. Staple to bind. Have your child decorate the pages with drawings, scribbles, or cutouts of images that they glue to the pages. Later, ask the child to tell you what's happening on

each page (the entire booklet may or may not have a narrative arc—that's fine!). At the bottom of the page, jot down what your child says about the illustrations. Keep these booklets with the library books and read them aloud to your children regularly. You might say, "Oh, look! Here's a book written by Mateo. Let's read it!"

* Retellings

Kids love to be experts. They'll tell you about their favorite television show or how they saw a red-tailed hawk swoop in the backyard. They might explain how to bathe a puppy. They might look at a work of art and declare, "I like the black lines that squiggle." Keep a record of these impromptu narrations. To retell is to make the information your own. By the end of a few months of jotting down these snippets of lively information, you'll have a nice cache of writing that represents your child's intellectual development!

* Lists

A fundamental writing skill is to be able to categorize information—to group like items, to make comparisons and contrasts between items, and so on. Your children are already good at this in speech. Use a notepad to create several lists as topics present themselves. Hang these lists on your refrigerator and add to them regularly. Here are a few list ideas to get you and your kids started: fruits that need to be peeled, birds at the bird feeder, songs we love to sing really loudly, favorite cartoons, names of each stuffed animal, birthday months, words that start with the same letter sound, rhyming words. You'll think of others. Once you start a list, reread it regularly and see if any new words come to your children's minds to add to it. Make this a collaborative project with all your kids.

PARTNERSHIP WRITING: EMERGING WRITERS (8–10)

Partnership Writing is probably the most overlooked (unused) stage of growth in a child's writing journey—and the most labor intensive. In most educational settings, kids are suddenly dropped off a cliff from barely reading and handwriting the alphabet to suddenly being asked to do all their own writing from scratch without help! That's not how kids gain independence in any other skill. It's perfectly appropriate to keep helping your child with writing. How you offer that help will gradually change over time as your child becomes more confident and competent. I hope this is good news for you. It will most certainly be good news for your child! Partnering with your child in their writing life starts with wordplay, scribbling and handwriting, and developing a point of view.

To put thoughts into writing, children have to be able to think at approximately the same pace as they handwrite or type. That's a tall order for anyone, but especially kids. Our role as the caring adult is to participate in the writing experience with our kids. Imagine weaning a child from bottle or breast. Initially, the adult controls the experience of eating, feeding the baby puree from a spoon. As the baby becomes a toddler, the little tyke grabs the spoon or mashes the banana with their own fists. They make a big mess on their way to being proficient self-feeders. That's as it should be! Over time, they gain more control over feeding themselves, and you provide less support (no more high chairs, bibs, special spoons, or puree).

Writing works the same way. We skip partnering with our children because we assume that providing any help to a young writer is "cheating." However, if you offer support corresponding to the need being presented, your child will grow more quickly as a writer and move into independence more easily. Once our kids are handwriting and reading a little, we give them the chance to put their own handwriting on the page. We might listen to a child eagerly talk about a topic. When the child picks up the pencil, we then dictate the child's own words back to them. The child writes their own words on the page. It's a two-step writing process on the way to a child transcribing their own thoughts directly, without that helpful middle step.

Partnership Writing is a season in which your fingerprints will be on the final version of the writing project. Sometimes you'll show your youngster how to do a little research. You might suggest topics for writing—narrowing the focus and expanding the writing in short bite-sized bits. You might show your youngster how to rhyme words or think of a title. That child might go with one of your suggestions. That's okay! The key goal of this stage is to put the pencil in your child's hand so that they are also writing; you are not the only transcriptionist anymore. Feel free to spell a word for your child or to point out when to capitalize or use a period. This is how your child learns—through conversations that feature kind, insightful guidance, while writing some of the words and sentences themselves.

During this stage of growth, children should continue to work on handwriting, begin to type (if they aren't already), and learn the typical conventions of punctuation. Spelling is important at this stage, but very difficult to master by age ten. (See chapter 11 for more thoughts on how to grow a child's spelling skills.) Many kids in this age range are ready to read chapter books by themselves, but don't forget the value of reading aloud. They love to hear you read and to listen to audiobooks—both. Playing audiobooks or reading to your child gives them a sense of intonation, inflection, and emotion. Hearing a book read aloud promotes reading comprehension as a result.

Your child may be in the Partnership Writing stage of growth if they have several of these characteristics:

* Can read

* Can handwrite

* Is learning to spell and punctuate

* Is eager to express themselves

* Can write a sentence or two without your help

* Needs support to keep writing

* Loves stories (in books or film)

✳ Shows resistance to writing from scratch

✳ Declares, "I hate writing!"

✳ Finds a new writing format daunting

✳ Becomes obsessed with facts about a favorite topic

Writing Activities for the Partnership Writing Stage

✳ **Paragraphs**

Your child is ready to write clusters of sentences at this stage. No need to drain the life out of their writing by imposing an artificial structure on the paragraph. Most children speak in paragraphs already. When they go to write, they will put those related thoughts on the page, frequently in a reasonably useful order. As you read their work with them, your task is to help your young writer notice when the topic *shifts* in a meaningful way. Show them that when the writing topic moves from one idea to another, it's time for a line break and an indentation to indicate a new paragraph.

Take a look at paragraphs in existing books, too, and notice the way the author chooses to group ideas. Some paragraphs are only a sentence or two! If your child writes a cluster of sentences and they seem out of order or there are too many ideas happening, try printing the cluster of sentences. Triple space them and then cut them up. Have your child rearrange the ideas in the best sequence, keeping the similar ideas together and removing sentences that don't belong. This is an imperfect process but an essential part of learning how to *think* about paragraphing. Traditional paragraph instructions require children to plan their content before writing and to change their content to suit a structure that doesn't necessarily encourage their best vocabulary, insight, or knowledge.

✱ Poetry

Poetic forms of all kinds—limericks, haiku, quatrains—are a fantastic way to grow writers in this stage. These forms impose a set of easy-to-follow rules that help children sort ideas and language to fit the appropriate patterns. Read lots of limericks over tea one day. Help your child write their own the next. Model how to pick a topic, how to hunt for rhyming words, how to think about telling a little story. Partnering in this project will mean that some of your ideas make it into the poem, which is A-OK. You could write limericks for a week as a way to see if your child catches on and begins to take more ownership over the process. Lots of poetry structures work with this age group. Keep the poetry to one stanza in length, and be sure to read samples of that exact structure before writing them.

* Letters

Composing an email, thank-you note, or letter to a friend is a great way to grow as a child writer. Letters can be handwritten or typed. They can be sent with a stamp or emailed. Penning a letter naturally puts the writer in their friendly, at-ease voice. Students have more access to their thoughts and ideas when they see the recipient as a friend or happy reader, rather than a teacher or vague audience. You can use letter writing to your child's academic advantage! Try it as the first step in writing a report.

Have your student write about the topic in a letter to someone they value (you, a grandparent, their other parent). Or they can write the report as a letter to a historical figure. Letter writing is not so much about the letter format as it is about putting your young writer at ease. If your child is supposed to write a four-paragraph report for school, have them write a letter to you about the topic first. Sometimes you can simply remove the salutation and the closing (signature), and you'll have a nice report ready to go!

BUILDING CONFIDENCE:
MIDDLE SCHOOL WRITING (11–12)

The Building Confidence stage of growth is the time when your child will alternate between feeling proud of their writing and never wanting to write again. Sometimes they'll have a sudden spurt of inspiration and write pages of fan fiction, and then the next week they won't be able to cough up two sentences about Disneyland. Your kids will weave in and out of enthusiasm for their writing assignments because they're still novice writers.

Imagine a child who loves to play and run. Just because that child knows how to run doesn't mean they're ready for marathons. Your kids are building stamina to write for longer periods of time and to work through all the steps of writing, from draft to polished paper. In addition, your tweens will not always show great spelling and punctuation skills in those drafts. They get better at spelling and punctuation during these years, but since they're only halfway on their journey to writing fluently, some notable errors will still pop through and surprise you (or infuriate you, if I'm honest). They'll get better and better at making corrections to their own writing, though.

During this stage of growth, your kids frequently find more uses for writing. They might get hooked on video game chat boards, or they may want to write scripts for short videos on social media. Some of your kids who were into dress-up clothes and playacting may switch to writing their own fan fiction. These bursts of creativity can be applauded and need no outside editing. See this kind of writing as the writerly version of playing "sword fight" or "The Little Mermaid." They use their writing to live in a world of their own imagination, to see what the story feels like, and to explore it in a patient, creative, and deliberate way. You don't need to worry about these stories having a beginning, middle, or end either. You wouldn't have expected dress-up play to fulfill a perfect story arc. Similarly, kids who write for pleasure use it as a tool for grown-up play. They aren't necessarily trying to write a full-fledged work of fiction. Instead, they use the power of language to spend happy time in their imaginations thinking about one scene. The gifts this personally motivated kind of writing brings to a middle school student are immeasurable. Be supportive. When one of your tweens asks you to read their self-motivated writing, give only positive feedback! This is not the time to use high-stakes revision strategies or to correct spelling and punctuation. Rather, your only job is to be amazed. Delight in the writing and the writer. The end.

Not all kids will write for pleasure, but most kids in this age range will wind up producing writing they like at some point. When they do, it's important to celebrate having written and then to take a break before the next writing activity or assignment. Writing is hard work. Everyone deserves orange slices and a little time to *not write.*

By middle school, your kids are ready to follow a format that eventually builds to the expository essays they'll write in high school. They can be taught how to sequence ideas and conduct research that gives them the details they need to support a point they want to make. They're ready to write their first drafts with less help from you. They're also ready to learn how to revise their writing after that draft is written (as discussed in chapter 9). If they gain these two skills and feel comfortable with both, they'll rock high school writing! Confidence in writing is built through success, pleasure, and taking more and more ownership of the writing process. This phase can last several years.

Your child may be in the Building Confidence stage of growth if they have several of these characteristics:

* Alternates between enjoying writing and
  resenting it

* Can type and handwrite comfortably

* Is able to start a draft without so much help from you

* Still makes some notable spelling and punctuation errors

* Writes for personal uses (like gaming chats, list making, or fan fiction)

* Still benefits from your support in research and revision processes

* Enjoys language in stories, jokes, facts, and conversation

Writing Projects for the Building Confidence Stage

* **Interviews**

There are two kinds of interviews students can conduct in this stage. The first is the most obvious sort—interviewing a living person that they know. This person could be an aging relative or their soccer coach or someone in a profession that interests them. Their goal is to solicit the kind of information they can translate from oral language into writing. The questions should be related to the writing topic. One popular angle I recommend for interviews is to find someone who was an eyewitness to a natural disaster. The sorts of questions the student asks will include factual detail and personal experience—two great sources of support when making points in expository writing. The second kind of interview I recommend is more like doing research. Choose an expert who can comment on the topic for writing. With your child, create a list of questions that you hope get answered about the topic when doing that research.

When your child reads an expert's opinion, have the student look for the kinds of comments that would answer some of those questions. This is a nice model for introducing the habit of research. By identifying questions they would ask a person if they could, your child guides their mind to read the material about the topic carefully, with an eye to getting answers from a source (expert). Put the interview questions on the page, spaced apart from each other, and have your student jot down the answers under the questions as they read and research, noting which source provided the answers.

* Literature Review

Middle school is a great time to learn how to analyze literature (not just to "report" about it). The goal is to select three to four literary devices to trace through the work of fiction. For instance, you might choose *foreshadowing, setting,* and *detailed descriptions.* Have your student jot notes that relate to those three aspects of literary analysis as they read the book. Put sticky notes on pages where those are found (three different colors of sticky notes help the student sort those incidences more easily too). At the end, write a five-paragraph summary (introduction, a paragraph each for the literary devices, and a concluding paragraph). To create this review, have your student freewrite about each literary device, one at a time, on separate sheets of paper. This strategy reduces the writing burden by spreading it out over a series of days. Then combine. Be sure to use the revision strategies in chapter 9 to polish it!

* The Five W's

Who, what, where, when, and why are excellent questions to ask about a historical event. At this age, kids can be guided to read and research using each question, one at a time. Take a sheet of paper. Turn it to be in landscape view and divide it into five columns. Put a *W* word at the top of each column. As the student reads or watches a documentary, take notes that fit under each of the columns. Freewrite on five sheets of paper over five days, one *W* at a time. Combine the freewrites to create a short report about the historical event. For a kicker, ask your child to offer an opinion in the final paragraph about the incident—how the incident has impacted the next phase in history, who was most impacted, how the way we see this event has changed over time, or some other viewpoint of analysis. Opinions are less about whether or not someone agrees with what happened and more about the implications of the event or series of events.

THE GREAT CONVERSATION: HIGH SCHOOL WRITING (13–14)

Welcome to the era of debate! High school students are ready for you. They want to test-drive all their feelings and thoughts (they call these "opinions") to see how adults react. Yet to develop a true opinion, the writer needs to know a good deal more about a topic than how their personal experience (organized with their own logic) relates to that topic.

Enter the expository essay. In high school, teachers want their students to transcend the temptation to make lazy arguments about the topics they study in class. The expository essay is a format designed to teach high schoolers how to structure an argument, conduct research, explore opposing views, and evaluate the claims of experts (among other things).

The expository essay format is not a joy to read, typically. In fact, ask yourself: When was the last time you read a high-school-style essay . . . for fun? Oh, never? Right. Most of us left that dusty old format in the waste bin in college and moved on to editorials and books for our nonfiction reading.

In academic life, the essay format lasts about eight years (high school and undergraduate work in college). In an eighty-year life, that's only ten percent of a full lifetime. So keep its relative importance in perspective. The essay offers instructors and professors an easy-to-evaluate format to see if their lessons in class "took." Expository essays are not necessarily masterpieces of writing craft, no matter who writes them!

One of the strange aspects of expository essay instruction is that students are expected to write essays before they've ever read them. Can you recall a time when a teacher handed out a set of essays to simply read? The answer I hear when I ask groups of adults that question is a resounding no. Most kids have a knack for writing ad copy (they know advertisement language and style better than almost any other writing format), fiction (they read novels), poetry (they sing song lyrics), reports (they've read textbooks, websites, and nonfiction books from the library), and humor (they read comic books and tell knock-knock jokes). When asked to use any of these formats in junior high writing, students have a good idea of how that format ought to sound. Yet once those same kids hit high school, those formats are tossed by the wayside and they're expected to write essays with no prior experience in reading essays. No wonder they feel intimidated!

The biggest gift you can give your high school students is finding a bunch of essays online and reading them together. Talk about the structure—the way the writer takes a position and supports it with points and particulars, such as expert opinion, data, research, experience, and logic. Notice the way those ideas are cited or woven into the text itself. Discuss whether or not the essay felt persuasive in the end or if there were any missing ideas that went unaddressed by the writer. If you do this with your students, they will have a leg up on the typical high school freshman.

Maybe you wonder why we call this bedrock academic format the "essay." The word *essay* comes from Latin, and it simply means "attempt" or "try." Wouldn't it be amazing if the rubric for grading an essay took that view? The teacher would read the essay and pose this question to themselves: "What is this student attempting to convey? What opinion is this student trying on for size? What academic effort do I see represented in this attempt to write an argument for this topic?" That, as you know, is not how essays are graded in school—but it can be how *you* respond to your child's essay writing. You can notice the attempts at complex logic or risky theories and ideas. You can applaud a student's efforts to organize the ideas into a neat and tight structure.

There are three key formats that students learn in high school that will form the foundation for all academic writing in college and likely graduate school too. The expository essay (often taught in the five-paragraph format first and then expanded to five or six pages), the timed essay (also known as the in-class essay), and the research paper (which usually runs between seven and thirty pages in length). There are dozens of twists on these formats—narrative, argumentative, exploratory, definition, compare and contrast, analysis and synthesis, informational, posing a solution, and more.

In this stage of academic development, the key to writing robust academic papers is knowing how to conduct the kind of reading and research that will populate those formats with insight. This is the stage of growth often called the Great Conversation. Students join a conversation in progress that spans the centuries. That conversation accounts for past achievements in the arts, humanities, and sciences, while interacting with the cutting-edge scholars and practitioners of this age. As students expand their studies in high school and college, they *eavesdrop* on that conversation. They're getting to know the key players in each field. They read the best writing, apply the most well-regarded theorems, and test the accepted research to understand how the story of that discipline came to be what it is today. By reading and writing about those topics with the guidance of an instructor, they learn the vocabulary and skills that are deemed necessary for participation.

The three key writing forms for academic writing serve as the tools for demonstrating mastery in those disciplines. Makes sense, right?

A student in the Great Conversation stage of growth may have several of these characteristics:

* Can competently write their own first drafts

* Understands how to improve their writing using some revision skills

* Reads widely

* Able to converse freely about what they read and what they're learning

* Can teach themselves vocabulary when they need to

* Shows interest in the opinions of others, not just their own (this is a work in progress, so don't despair if this one is inconsistently expressed!)

* Uses internet search engines competently

* Able to apply critical thinking to what they read and research

Writing Projects for The Great Conversation Stage

✳ Online Writing

Finding online spaces to test-drive opinions and ideas is a great plan for this age. Brave Writer offers online writing classes that encourage this kind of free exploration of thinking and writing. They mirror the kind of online platforms colleges use with students too. Some discussion boards or writing communities offer a similar experience to students of this age. You can also cultivate this skill with your kids by using a family chat program; apps like WhatsApp and Slack can be wonderful tools for this kind of written conversation. Think of provocative topics and use the online tool to discuss in an informal, conversational way. Resist the temptation to direct or guide the conversation. Rather, post links to articles or data or research about a topic your teen likes, and then discuss it, referencing the content of those sources. (For more help, try using my teen workbook called *Becoming a Critical Thinker* as a tool to help all of you learn how to grow in critical thinking through writing.)

✳ Personal Writing

School will give your students a shot at the formats. It's up to you to protect personal writing with your early teens. Dr. Peter Elbow recommends a kind of writing he calls the "think piece." It's a little more directed than a freewrite, but not as well constructed as an essay. The idea goes like this. Identify a provocative idea or question that the student finds compelling. Jot it down at the top of a sheet of paper or online document. Set a timer for fifteen to twenty minutes. Write about the topic, exploring all the aspects of it that come to mind during that time period. Try writing as though you agree with the suggested premise. Then switch and write as though you disagree. Explore solutions and obstructions. Consider impacts and benefits. Write, write, write.

In Brave Writer, we use the "think piece" structure to explore literature. We pose specific questions about a work of fiction and then have the student write a think piece to address the question. When we ask students to write about *Pride and Prejudice*, for example, one of our think piece questions is: "Social class played a large role in the lives of everyone living during the Regency Era in England. Just as Elizabeth is aware that she has an inferior ranking to Mr. Darcy, Miss Bingley makes it clear that she has a superior ranking to Elizabeth. What is Miss Bingley's role in the novel? What group of people does she represent, according to Austen? What can you conclude about how Austen views social hierarchy?" The goal is to explore each of these ideas freely in writing, without regard to structuring an argument.

* Essays

There's no way around it. Your teens will write essays—short ones, timed ones, and long ones that become research papers. For your reluctant writers, start by reading essays. Use online search to find essay samples written by teens. Read them together and analyze what works, what doesn't, and how they are constructed. Use the tools of "reader response feedback" to analyze these essays. When your child goes to write their first essay, be sure to be your child's partner, coach, and ally. You can offer help guilt-free, and you'll see your student learn to write essays much more quickly if you participate. (See chapter 12 for tips about how to use AI when writing essays and conducting research too.) Remember: early attempts at essay writing will sound wooden. Think of the essay format a bit like training wheels on a bike. Writers have to get the feel of the structure before they can make it their own.

RHETORICAL IMAGINATION: COLLEGE PREP WRITING (15–18)

I like to call this next stage of growth in writing the Rhetorical Imagination stage. This is the time in a teen's life when they learn to imagine viewpoints they don't hold. In the same way your children attempted to playact characters, teens can now inhabit a point of view to try it on for size. Lots of teens get this chance through performing a character in a play production in high school and learning to inhabit the character's beliefs and motivations. By acting, they get to try on a different point of view to understand it from the inside. This is the key developmental skill teens need to become high-quality thinkers.

By their mid-teens, students develop the ability to bring skillful analysis to their thinking. At first, they'll be clunky thinkers, the same way they were messy eaters when they first used a fork and spoon. It's tricky to wield the tools of logic and argument, correlating facts with a viewpoint, analyzing data, and recognizing when that same data is being manipulated. This is the time when your teens consider what constitutes justice and injustice, what it means to write about the historical record, and how scientific advancement is both beneficial and harmful. Don't be surprised if your teens adopt a viewpoint you don't hold as they work through the implications of their beliefs. That's natural and is not necessarily permanent. Your teen may go vegan or become a pacifist or turn to religion—even if these are not your family's beliefs. All of it is in service of growing a mind.

These are the years students spend honing their writing skills, too, particularly the skills of revision and editing. They can be counted on to do a deeper read through of their own writing, with an understanding of how to improve it. They'll take greater responsibility for ensuring that the final draft is error-free. Students at this age will do the same kind of writing they started earlier in high school—the essay, timed essay, and research paper formats. Now they'll add a new writing format to their tool kit—the autobiographical narrative essay. This is the one they'll use to apply to college, in fact! They may branch out and write poetry, song lyrics, and/or fiction, and develop websites too.

You know your student is in the Rhetorical Imagination stage of growth if they have some of these characteristics:

* Is capable of writing a five-paragraph essay (and is either a junior or senior in high school)

* Reads widely and has access to a variety of sources about the ideas of our time

* Likes to hold big juicy conversations with you and online with friends

* Is capable of taking positions about ideas that matter to them

* Is often college bound

By the time you have kids this age and with this level of skill, you'll be less necessary to the overall writing process. That said, every now and then it's really valuable to step in and provide plenty of support.

Support Strategies for the Rhetorical Imagination Stage

* Go out for Cokes and discuss your kids' classes and what they're learning. If you can read some of what they read (books, texts, articles, online research), your conversations will be richer. What kids need at this age is high-caliber dialogue partners. Your task is to ask questions that provoke new thinking, not to indoctrinate them into your thinking. Resist the urge to correct an opinion. Instead, ask the kinds of questions that help the teen dig a little deeper. For ideas of what kinds of questions to ask, see my book

Raising Critical Thinkers. There's a chapter on the "Rhetorical Imagination" with a slew of questions to ask.

* Offer to type while your child dictates their thoughts to you. At this stage of development, the thoughts can sometimes be a bit of a linguistic jumble. Typing and thinking is hard again. Help your teen by allowing them to put all their attention on talking while you give them support through typing. Alternatively, they can use voice-to-text software.

* Be the kind reader they need when they get that draft written. Start with reader-response feedback that is encouraging and supportive. Notice what works. Once you've expressed what works well and what you liked, *ask* your teen if they're open to the "narrow and expand" kind of feedback described in chapter 9. If they are, highlight two or three places where the writing would benefit from *more* writing. Remember: your job isn't to argue but to pose questions that prompt more writing. You might say, "I'm interested in knowing *more* about the opposing viewpoint. How do you account for X?" This is a respectful way to ask for a deeper dive into the controversy at the heart of an essay without saying, "This is illogical. Don't you know that the other side says X?"

* Help them apply to college. It's difficult to do it alone. You can take them on college visits, look at

the application together, and work on the autobiographical essay. Remember to read lots of those essays before you work on it together. The key to this essay is to make it personal and relevant to the experience the student wants to get out of college.

Writing Projects for the Rhetorical Imagination Stage
Reluctant or resistant teen writers may struggle with some key skills that make writing easier. You can focus on those using these ideas at home.

* **Paraphrasing, Summarizing, and Citing Sources**
  One of the biggest challenges teens face is learning how to take the language of an expert and put it into their own words. This skill is especially tricky if your teen is reading about a topic that is unfamiliar to them. Start by picking a topic that is a passion of your teen's, like a favorite band or streaming show. Have your teen read reviews. Ask your teen to take two different opinions (one that is positive and one that is negative) and put them into their own words. Paraphrases usually match the length of the original quote, more or less. For a summary, the writer reduces the length of the quote to get to the main issues. Give both a whirl! Last, you can also practice taking the quote and putting it into a sentence using the proper punctuation and citation method (lots of online tools show you how to craft a citation).

* Embodying a Viewpoint

It's difficult to accept a viewpoint that contradicts a strongly held belief. One way to be fair to a view you don't hold is to imagine the kind of person who holds that viewpoint. Rachel Kadish, author of the novel *The Weight of Ink*, teaches a valuable practice to her student writers. She recommends that students write down a phrase they would find upsetting in some way—it could be a personal attack or a slogan that describes someone's viewpoint about a social issue. Students are directed to create a fictional character who believes in this view. She then advises students to write a monologue in first person defending that belief—including the backstory that might inform that viewpoint. Through this process, she's seen students develop, at minimum, greater understanding and, at maximum, new empathy for a worldview that differs from their own. In the same way playacting allows a student to embody a view they don't hold, this writing practice can offer students a way to investigate a perspective they would feel uncomfortable adopting. This kind of writing activity is likely to go best if you try it as well!

* Writing for Pleasure

It's easy to lose sight of writing as a tool for self-expression or self-awareness. Sometimes that means putting pen to the page. Other times, it could mean dictating thoughts to a voice-to-text app. One college student I met told me he uses a private version of ChatGPT where he records his thoughts regularly. He's able to then use that AI tool to investigate the themes he returns to, embedded ideas he missed, and trends in how he thinks about his major and future career. Private writing is the place where students can examine their conscience, their feelings, their difficult experiences, and their bright ideas for the future. Developing a regular private writing practice, even if using voice-to-text, is a wonderful gift to give students at this age.

IT ALL ADDS UP TO LEARNING

The last stage of growth in writing is a competent, confident adult writer! That's the kind of person who can write emails, business reviews, reports, letters, scathing rebukes on social media, detailed engineering records, and more. That is likely you. It can be your kids too.

YOUR WRITING ASSIGNMENT

Reflect on where your child is currently on the timeline of writing fluency. How can you support that child's development as they move into the next phase? Pick one activity to try with your child and jot that down.

|||||||||||||||||||||||

CHAPTER 11

Spelling, Punctuation, and Grammar

This book is about kids who hate writing. Many of them hate it not because they dislike expressing themselves but because they struggle with spelling, punctuation, and grammar. And no matter how much I might try to persuade you that spelling, punctuation, and grammar are relatively unimportant to the overall success of your young writers, I know you worry anyway. That's to be expected. Nothing signals "being dumb" in the eyes of the unkind public more than making spelling and grammar mistakes. It's completely unfair and wrong, but nevertheless, it's reality. Many of us bear the scars of criticism, whether from friends, family, schoolteachers, or anonymous online trolls. It's cruel and unnecessary, but I'm not likely to change the entire culture's attitudes about the standards of written English in a few paragraphs, so let's face the issue head-on.

My first goal with this chapter is to remind you of the writer who lives inside your child. Their quirky, unique thoughts belong to them and matter, no matter how they're spelled or punctuated. My second goal is to relieve you of the feeling of failure that pings you when you see your child has misspelled the same word for the fifth time or put the comma in the wrong place yet again. With that in mind, let's figure out how to know when a kid needs extra help and what to do to ensure that your child is continuing to improve their transcription skills over time.

SPELLING

Despite the rigorous perfectionism we impose on everyone, spelling is not a perfect and logical system handed down from on high, especially not in English. English spelling, like the English language itself, is a hodgepodge of words with origins in many different languages that have many different approaches to phonics (the way we use written letters to represent the spoken sounds of words). For instance, think of the slew of sounds the spelling *-ough* can make in words like *thought, rough, bough, slough, though,* and *cough.* And that's just in American spelling—in British spelling, you could add *plough* and *hiccough* to the list. (The very fact that there are differences between American and British spelling is yet another indicator that English spelling is not always rational or consistent.) By the way, did you notice I just used two words— *slew* and *slough*—that are pronounced the same but spelled differently? English spelling is rife with homophones like this. Two plus two always equals four, but the same written letters can indicate half a dozen different sounds and vice versa. Of course that's hard to learn at first!

Today, there are dictionaries and language standards that we apply to everyone, but we forget that there was a time not so long ago when there were *no* standardized spellings. People used whatever phonics they had, and words were spelled in numerous acceptable ways. You may have heard of this guy William Shakespeare—or should we write it, like he did, as Shakespear, Shakspere, or Shaksper? Yes, he spelled his own name multiple ways, because consistent spelling simply wasn't considered an important part of mastering the English language at the time.

The point is: being able to spell well has nothing to do with being an intelligent person or a good writer. We have to let go of feeling like it's a moral failure when a child misspells a word. It's not! It hardly matters. As I've emphasized throughout this book, the mechanics of writing are a separate skill from producing original writing. As we move into a brave new world of more and more advanced technology, it's hard to know if students of the future will have to write anything with their own hands at all. Until that time, however, learning and using standardized spelling makes you the most effective transcriptionist of your thoughts—and helps ward off judgment from teachers and the horde of insensitive internet users who notice any errant letter.

So how do we help our kids do that?

To be a good speller, a child needs to know how to read—and well. Be sure to use a phonics-based program that is built from the science of reading. Today there's a robust debate between two approaches to teaching reading—a phonics-based approach versus a "whole language" approach. Without diving into that argument here, the important insight from that debate is that students need a solid foundation in phonics instruction to ensure their best chance at fluency and competent spelling.

When your child gets a spelling wrong, the first step I recommend is to identify whether they're making a random guess, attempting to use a known phonetic strategy, or just mixing up two homophones. If a child writes *threw* but means *through*, for example, that's not a spelling error per se. They're using a correct spelling for a real word, but it happens to be the wrong word for the context. You can validate that the spelling is accurate for a word with a different meaning, then expand your child's understanding by explaining that there's a homophone with the meaning they had in mind. By validating the correctness of the spelling, you preserve the child's sense of being smart. You then help them evaluate their writing to see if they are using the *right* words for the *right* contexts. This is a powerful editing skill to develop.

One way to work on this skill is to craft sentences that use both homophones in them. Leave the homophones out and have your child fill in the right word in the right context while listening to you read the sentence aloud. For example: *Billy* _____ *the ball* _____ *the window.* (You'd say, "Billy **threw** the ball **through** the window.") Giving your child a chance to listen to the two similar-sounding words near to each other in a meaningful context helps them think about which one to pick when the sound of that word pops into their minds. Homophone dictation practice is a great way to grow these skills.

Sometimes kids might spell a word in a logical but incorrect way. Imagine your child writes the word "vacashun" instead of "vacation." The phonics make perfect sense. It's just that we don't spell that word that way. You can affirm your child's use of phonics: "Yes, those are all the letter sounds that match the word. Here's how we actually spell it: vacation. The 'tion' makes the /shun/ sound." Conversation with this sort of explanation takes the sting out of a misspelling.

Once in a while, a bilingual child will mix up the phonetic systems of two languages. I remember a friend's daughter wrote an entire page of paragraphs with countless misspellings after she moved back to the States from Morocco. When I looked over her writing, it was apparent that the English words all obeyed French phonetics! Once I pointed that out to her, she made the shift on her own to using the right phonetic system for the corresponding language.

In chapter 9, Johannah's diary revealed several misspellings, including her attempt to spell "diamonds," which she wrote as "dimons." This isn't quite phonetically accurate, but she's got the essential sounds that we say when we speak the word naturally. Most people don't say "di-ah-mondz." To learn to spell that word correctly will take a little conversation. It might help to exaggerate the sounds while handwriting it. Some kids need to practice copying a word while saying the sounds aloud (one sound per letter or cluster of letters) as they handwrite or type the corresponding letters to solidify the correct spelling.

If your kids or teens are still struggling with spelling skills, especially if they have a learning disability like dyslexia or dysgraphia, it's important to work with a specialist who can provide the right kinds of therapies. It doesn't matter how old your child is. The intervention of a specialist can be an absolute rescue for a child who feels "dumb." When my son was helpfully tutored to address his dysgraphia, for example, I was introduced to the practice of sounding out the word as the child writes the letters. The child doesn't say the *name* of the letter but rather the *sounds* that make the word as their pencil is writing the corresponding letters. That means sometimes the writer will say the sounds the word makes as they are writing letters that seem to be silent. For instance, if your child were to write "knock," the /n/ sound is made by both the *k* and the *n* together. The child would say the /n/ sound out loud as they write the *kn* and then shift to the /o/ sound as they handwrite the letter *o*. By coordinating the hand with the sounds, your child encodes the spellings that correspond with those sounds. If you're working with a child at home, expect a noisy spelling lesson!

Should kids be allowed to use the spell check feature in a word processor or web browser while they're still learning to spell? There's some controversy about this. My solution? Yes, sometimes. At times it's good to push yourself to have to spell using your own mind to remember the letter order. Other times, spell check provides the spelling right when you wonder about it. I know for myself, some of my "hangers on" (words I habitually misspelled) have gone away because of spell check. (I now know that there are two *c*'s and two *m*'s in *accommodate*!) I'm also a big believer in the idea that when a child asks for a spelling, you can call it back to them to help, in the same way you would if your spouse shouted, "Hey honey, how do you spell *ridiculous* again?" No one wants to be sent to a dictionary.

Spelling Tests

Spelling tests are one of the most common tools we use when teaching spelling, but sometimes it seems like they don't work.

A child can memorize spellings for a test, but when they go to use those same exact words in the context of their own writing, they may misspell them. Parents often ask me what's going on when that happens. What researchers have learned is that memorizing words in a list uses the pattern-seeking part of the brain. The child can put these patterns to use when they take a test that isolates particular words that have a spelling convention in common. However, when a student is asked to write from scratch, if they haven't mastered a particular spelling in the context of meaningful language, they may forget the correct spelling. That writer is focused on their thoughts (a sequence of ideas) and not the pattern of the letters.

It takes time for a student to be able to manage both the spelling and the meaning of a word simultaneously. Until they do so, they'll find it difficult to spell every word accurately while also thinking freely enough to write. This is why some kids say, "I can't write because I'm afraid of misspelling a word." What they're telling you is that they're distracted from the task of producing original writing by being ill at ease with spelling. One way to get past this particular struggle is to remind them that they can use any version of spelling that comes to mind in a freewrite, but then before they show their writing to you, they'll have the chance to go back through and put all their attention on how to spell the words they wrote. They can correct spellings *after* they write but *before* you see their work. They may still overlook a few misspellings, but it is this habit of checking over their own work that leads them to greater and greater skill in spelling.

Not every pedagogy believes in spelling tests. There are two key practices often used in England and France that teach spelling without lists and tests. These practices are called *copywork* and *dictation*, and they're an important part of the Brave Writer curriculum. Let me express the main ideas here.

Copywork is the practice of copying a beautiful piece of writing in your own handwriting (or typing it into a document on a computer). By reading the words in context and putting them in your own hand, you help your brain coordinate the spellings it observes with the meaning the words generate. The practice simulates what it's like to think a thought and write it out too.

The second practice, dictation, works like this: the teacher or parent reads a beautiful passage of writing aloud, and the students transcribe it on their own sheets of paper as they listen. Unlike copywork, the child has no visual reference for the passage. Dictation allows a child to hear fluent language and to apply the rules of spelling and punctuation to it in a similar way to how they would transcribe their own thoughts into writing. The difference is that because that student doesn't also have to think of the thoughts, they can give full attention to how the words should be spelled and punctuated. Having used spelling and punctuation in a meaningful context, when the student goes to write from scratch, they're more able to retrieve the appropriate spellings and punctuation marks. The French *love* their dictation practices! In June of 2023, five thousand French adults signed up to perform a world-record-breaking group "dictée" on the Champs Élysées in front of the Arc de Triomphe. When I studied abroad in France as a college student, we practiced dictation in all my classes.

These practices, if adopted regularly, teach spelling and punctuation effectively. Not only that, copywork and dictation can be a really lovely experience. Kids get to pick passages from books they enjoy reading and can keep this written rec-

ord of their favorite quotes. Brave Writer also has several programs that teach these practices to students of all ages.

PUNCTUATION

What we often forget about punctuation is that it's a set of
symbols much the same way letters are a set of symbols. You
have to be able to read and understand these symbols in order
to apply them correctly to your own writing. As a parent or
teacher, you may be so busy teaching your kids to read the alphabet you forget that they're also learning to read a system of
dots, curves, and lines that don't make sounds on their own.
When kids read, they're often so fluent in English that they
automatically supply the inflection the punctuation is meant
to convey without really noticing those little markings on the
page. In order to teach punctuation to children, it's important
to make the punctuation *stand out* so that they notice it.

To help kids notice a given punctuation mark, I recommend using it incorrectly at first. For instance, what if you
want to show the impact of commas? Begin by removing the
commas from a sentence and read it aloud that way, without
the appropriate pauses.

Here's a sample sentence: *After a long nap, the dog played
with his ball, a length of rope, and an old rag doll.*

First, remove the commas: *After a long nap the dog played
with his ball a length of rope and an old rag doll.*

Read it fast without pausing. How does that sound?

Next, add lots of commas to the sentence. Put one behind
every word: *After, a, long, nap, the, dog, played, with, his, ball,
a, length, of, rope, and, an, old, rag, doll.*

Now read the same sentence aloud, obeying the commas

by pausing after each word. How does that sound? Weird, right?

Have your children read along on their own papers or by looking at the whiteboard. Let them experience the impact that the presence and absence of commas make on reading. After you've tried reading the sentence both ways, read it again with commas in the right places, obeying the pauses the commas indicate. When you return to the sentence with commas in the appropriate spots, kids are bound to notice!

Try the same thing with punctuation marks that go at the end of a sentence. Imagine swapping periods for question marks and reading every sentence as a question. Then do the same with exclamation points. Then randomly mix them up and see how it feels to read a sentence that way! Play, play, play with punctuation before you expect a child to use it correctly. By using punctuation in "wrong" ways, you give your kids a chance to experience the markings as meaningful because they alter how a child intonates a sentence.

The more you play with the tools of punctuation in ways that aren't natural, the more you help your kids *see* and then *hear* the inflections those marks are meant to indicate when they are used properly. We spend so much time telling kids how something ought to be used before they experience it for themselves. By doing a little violence to the original uses, you help kids feel the direct meaningful impact of those marks.

Another way to encourage attention to punctuation is to hand your child a photocopied page from a book they're currently reading. Give them a set of highlighters. Ask them to highlight each punctuation mark they see. Then ask them to explain to you why it's there. They'll have to think about the choices the author made and attempt to rationalize those choices to you. This kind of intentional attention to punctuation helps your kids become more aware of the power of those dots, curves, and lines too. You might notice, for instance, that your child never highlights apostrophes. That would be a great opportunity to talk about how this little curved mark sits above the words it modifies. You can then talk about the difference between when an apostrophe indicates a possessive and when it indicates a contraction. By having a big juicy conversation around punctuation, you help your kids *notice* the marks to begin with and then see them as meaningful tools for their own writing.

GRAMMAR

As I've mentioned in previous chapters, every child (except for those with certain learning disabilities) speaks naturally and fluently in their native language, following the rules of grammar used in their community, with a flawless local accent by the time they're five. Grammar—the way a language is organized and structured—is intuitive to native speakers. They know grammar "by ear," not by rules. If they want to make a sentence, they ask themselves if what they are about to say "sounds right." They don't ask if they should conjugate the verb in the past tense.

Not so with non-native language speakers! If you've ever studied Spanish or Arabic, you know that when you start out, the only way you can get close to how the language is supposed to sound is by applying *rules* to the sentences you form. When learning a second language, understanding grammar is essential to progress in fluency. This can also be true for those who grow up in communities that use nondominant versions of English. These are perfectly valid forms of language and deserve to be honored as such, and it's important to encourage children to write in these kinds of English in some contexts. But when learning the conventions of standard written English, these students may find it helpful to consciously think about grammar the way they would have when learning another language.

The point is: to learn about the grammar of a language you're already fluent in is a wildly tricky journey. On the one hand, you know how everything should sound. On the other hand, you don't necessarily know why. Studying grammar can be an exciting way to examine one's own language, but it has very little to do with writing from scratch. The native speaker ought to rely on their natural voice when writing. That will be the best source of words that feel familiar in the writer's hands.

I recommend studying conventional English grammar in that "curious about how language is built" way three times in a child's life.

1. Introduce the parts of speech during elementary school. Play with nouns, verbs, adjectives, adverbs, and prepositions.

2. In junior high, introduce the notion of sentence structure—how words collaborate to create meaning in the form of sentences, fragments, paragraph structure, and more.

3. In high school, study another language. By learning a new language, your child will automatically backdate that understanding of grammar to their own language.

For writing, the most important aspect of grammar is being able to notice when you swap homonyms, misuse apostrophes (because how they are used identifies which word and meaning you intend), or how well you can adapt your spoken English to the academic conventions of written English (for instance, if you write "Her and me" as the subject of a sentence because that's how you speak, you'll want to know to correct it to "She and I" in most academic writing contexts). Two of my favorite books that address these native speaker malaprops are *Woe Is I* and *Eats, Shoots & Leaves*.

TRAIN THE EARS AND EYES

To become comfortable with both original writing and the transcription skills of spelling, punctuation, and grammar, I recommend six steps.

1. **Read aloud to your child.** Reading aloud tunes a child's ear to fluent written language. Picture books, nonfiction, novels, billboards, recipes, instructions for a video game, comics, websites—read aloud intentionally and as a natural part of your day so that your child hears a variety of writing styles. Audiobooks count.

2. **Have your child read to themselves.** By reading to themselves, your child is training their eyes to see punctuation and spellings in context. Today it can be difficult to get a child to sit still to read to themselves. Here are a couple of tips. Host a "reading to self" time of the day where parents and kids all

cozy up with a book they're reading. The television, phones, and other devices are off. Another option is to give your kids reading material at bedtime. Let them read in bed until they're ready to sleep. For struggling readers, have them read aloud to you a bit each day. You might alternate reading paragraphs with them to provide some support. Another idea is to have them follow along in a book while they listen to the audiobook. Some parents have found that keeping closed captions on while watching TV also supports reading growth.

3. **Invite your child to investigate a passage, noticing punctuation and spellings.** Have your child give full attention to a few sentences in a book, noticing the punctuation marks and identifying any spellings that seem challenging to read. Have conversations about the words and punctuation marks. Being deliberate about noticing helps a child feel empowered—they're applying their own mind to think about what interests or provokes them.

4. **Practice applying what is being learned through copywork and dictation.** These tools are powerful in helping a child pair the meanings of the words they're writing with the transcription skills to support clarity and accuracy.

5. **Have your child take the first pass to edit and correct their own errors.** By encouraging your child to read their own writing first, you shift the respon-

sibility for a clean edit to the child so that they learn to notice their habits. They may not find all their mistakes, but they will become more comfortable noticing some of them and correcting them.

6. **Last, include freewriting as a regular practice**. Your child will coordinate their thoughts and skills in freewriting. They can edit that freewrite using the principles outlined in chapter 8 to apply what they're learning about spelling, punctuation, and grammar. You will see what they still don't know how to do reliably and can make a note of what to explore and learn in the next week.

Curricula like Brave Writer can support you in this journey to fluency in writing with explicit writing activities and assignments that will transform your children's writing experience and skill.

YOUR WRITING ASSIGNMENT

You've come a long way in this writing journey with your kids. Use your writing notebook to make notes about which activities you intend to try with your kids! Remember: you can start with just one. No need to be overwhelmed— simply start with the concept or practice that caught your attention.

||||||||||||||||||||||

CHAPTER 12

Artificial Intelligence and Writing

We began this book asking the question: Why write? I answered it by saying that we write for ourselves first and for readers second. I want to add a third reason we write: to learn. Writing helps us to put the raw unedited ideas in our minds onto a page or screen. We discover how well we know what we know when we try to write about it, and we gain more knowledge as we take the time to do additional research or think more deeply about our topic in order to write about it more thoughtfully.

Today, in the age of artificial intelligence, this third reason to write may be under threat. Everywhere you turn, artificial intelligence seems to be encroaching on—usurping?—the skills and talents humans have brought to the table for thousands of years. It's understandable that we're all a little skittish. Will the next generation of children opt out of writing and, therefore, learning? It's time to talk about ChatGPT and all the implications of the artificial intelligence programs currently on the rise.

ARTIFICIAL "INTELLIGENCE"

In the same way I know you worry your eleven-year-old is scribbling any old set of letters on the page instead of learning to spell correctly, it's likely you're worried that your seventeen-year-old is relying too much on ChatGPT when writing their high school papers. If you're like lots of parents today, you may worry that your teens aren't going to learn to write or think because they're being seduced by a technology that pretends to be human. (Sounds like a bad sci-fi movie!) Artificial intelligence is challenging all of our assumptions about what it means to be an educated and skillful writer.

But what precisely do we mean by "artificial intelligence"? The term can encompass a wide variety of technologies, but we usually use it to refer to applications that use complicated networks of algorithms to "learn" on their own, without explicit programming instructions dictating their every move. As they're "trained" on huge amounts of data that an individual human could never process, they become increasingly good at making accurate predictions, analyzing complex problems, and more, with little additional input from humans. Some of AI's feats are astonishing, but we still have to put words like "learn" and "train" in quotes, because, even though these algorithmic "neural networks" are often modeled after our understanding of how our own neurons work, they don't yet come close to rivaling a real brain's complexity. Despite its name, artificial intelligence is not truly intelligent or conscious the way a person is.

As I write this, the poster child for AI is ChatGPT, one of several similar AI-driven chatbots currently on the market. The G in GPT stands for "generative," and whether or not this particular app stands the test of time, it's a safe bet that generative AI—any AI that can generate its own original text, images, music, or other content—will be relevant for the foreseeable future. ChatGPT uses what is called a large language model (LLM) to create text. An LLM trains on an enormous dataset (like the whole World Wide Web) to become extremely skillful at predicting what comes next in a string of words. If you start texting someone and type "How are," your phone might suggest that the next thing you type should be "you?," because, by the numbers, that's what's most likely to come next. LLMs do the same thing but at a very advanced level, "learn[ing] patterns and relationships in the text data . . . to create humanlike responses by predicting what text should come next in any given sentence."

A GPT's goal is to respond to a prompt with information written in language that mimics the natural cadence of a fluent native speaker—and it usually succeeds. It was startling to me to realize that ChatGPT doesn't actually *understand* English (or any language, since it's not a conscious mind). Instead, it follows a very detailed map of how concepts relate to each other and uses that map to predict what words are most likely to follow. For instance, when I asked ChatGPT to define the literary device called "alliteration," it did a great job. When I asked it to find Taylor Swift song lyrics that showcase alliteration, it did an abysmal job! I got a set of popular Taylor Swift lyrics but none that were discernibly alliterative. AI is both ingenious and stupid at the same time.

Is this explanation above your pay grade too? It's a lot to

take in if you're not a computer scientist. Here's what's important for us to understand about AI in the context of teaching writing, however. While a GPT can predict the next word or sentence or paragraph, and it has scoured the internet to train and learn, it cannot think. It doesn't generate original thought. The best it can do is synthesize the thinking that human beings have published online.

When you pose a question or enter a prompt, the AI program is "trained" to give you an answer that creates the experience of participating in a dialogue with someone knowledgeable and trustworthy. The trouble is this: ChatGPT is not designed to vet the facts it drums up or to determine what is accurate and what is false. In the absence of a fact, AI will do what it always does: predict which words would most likely come next. If that prediction is wrong, it results in what is called a "hallucination": false information stated by an AI that sounds credible but is only superficially similar to true, verifiable information—like my Taylor Swift example above.

A newsworthy example of this happened in December 2023. In a high-profile legal case, Michael Cohen (the former personal lawyer for President Donald Trump) and his lawyers filed a motion citing legal precedent that didn't exist. Cohen had used Bard (now renamed Gemini), an AI chatbot similar to ChatGPT made by Google, to help write the motion, and it "hallucinated" legal decisions that hadn't actually happened. Cohen claimed that he didn't know artificial intelligence would invent case law that didn't exist. His team didn't even bother to fact-check the GPT.

These hallucinations are typical of AI. Dr. Kelly Cohen, director of the AI Biolab at the University of Cincinnati (and no relation to Michael Cohen), says that as of February 2024, there are nearly 1.7 million hallucinations per day created through ChatGPT alone. By some estimates, about 15 to 20 percent of ChatGPT's output is hallucinations. The bottom line is, no matter how impressive its capabilities, AI is not to be trusted for perfect accuracy.

AI AS A TOOL

In February 2024, Marley Stevens, a college student at University of North Georgia, proofread a paper using Grammarly, an app that makes use of AI to help fix spelling, grammar, and punctuation errors but doesn't generate original text the way ChatGPT does. Her professor ran the paper through Turnitin, a plagiarism-detection app that also uses AI. Turnitin flagged that Stevens had used Grammarly but also indicated that part of the paper was created through generative AI (AI that creates original content from scratch à la ChatGPT). Stevens says she didn't use generative AI, and indeed, it has been demonstrated that AI detectors are notoriously flawed, picking up AI where it wasn't used and missing it where it was. Not exactly ironclad proof of cheating, yet Stevens received a zero and was put on academic probation until 2025. Welcome to the circus that is "catching students cheating"—the worst kind of educational environment.

As debates rage about how AI, and particularly Large Language Models, will impact education, high schools and universities are grappling with which protocols to establish for paper writing and test taking. The truth is: we're in a brand-new world. Is our best strategy to use shame, penalties, and AI detectors to catch our kids in the act of using the latest beneficial technology? Or is it to learn to play nicely with AI? Soheil

Feizi, the director of University of Maryland's Reliable AI Lab, takes the position that I advocate: "A more comprehensive solution is to embrace the AI models in education. It's a little bit of a hard job, but it's the right way to think of it. The wrong way is to police it and, worse than that, rely on unreliable detectors in order to enforce that."

Of course we don't want students to misuse AI, but we don't want to misuse it ourselves either. How can students and educators alike learn to use AI as a useful tool rather than a shortcut to get out of work or a weapon to punish students who may not even have done anything wrong?

In Dr. Kelly Cohen's engineering classes at University of Cincinnati, he teaches what he calls "responsible, ethical AI." He begins by telling his students that using AI to create projects or write papers is permitted, but if there is a single hallucination in their work—a single statistic or data point or reference that isn't real—they receive a failing grade immediately. He's more concerned that the data and analysis are both accurate and make the points the student wants to make than whether each word in that paper was thought of from scratch by the student. To his way of thinking, the assist that AI provides in writing is on par with the way graphing calculators transformed mathematics in the late twentieth century. Graphing calculators enabled mathematics and engineering students to focus on higher-level problem-solving rather than slogging through more rudimentary calculations. In a way, calculators let mathematicians focus on the business of mathematics.

For writing, GPTs can play a similar role. Learning how to generate a prompt that guides the GPT to give you the information you need is one of the first thinking skills a student must cultivate in order to effectively use a GPT. Crafting those prompts requires a student to sift through the writing assignment for its key ideas, distill those ideas into questions, and then pose them in a way the GPT can use to offer relevant information. The student needs to know enough about the topic to direct the GPT. If a student chooses to use a GPT like an essay generator, they will be using it in the same way a college student pays a roommate to write their history paper. But if a student knows how to guide it, they can use a GPT like a coach at the college writing lab—as a brainstorming partner and editor.

Lots of kids struggle with the initial burst of writing needed to begin a longer paper. What the GPT can do is help the student immediately address the topic in smaller chunks. If you think back to the revision chapters in this book, you'll recall that one of the strategies for writing *more* is to narrow the focus (to one paragraph or one idea) and then to expand the writing—focusing on just that part of the topic. In a similar way, a GPT puts the student into a mindset that helps them narrow their focus to expand the writing. Once a student sees words populating the screen, a kind of relief often sets in. Now the student has words to read, to vet, and to revise. The skilled writing student will take that raw material from the GPT offering and make it their own. For people who find the blank page and blank screen especially intimidating, this is great news!

I recently attended a meetup for a cohort of people in the field of education and business in Cincinnati interested in the future of artificial intelligence. Together, they are collaborating to establish ethical guidelines for the responsible use of AI in education and the workplace. This is the right way to think about this powerful technology. Human beings can govern how AI and GPTs are used, if we have the collective will to create those regulations (like we've had to with the advent of motor vehicles). Even if we feel nervous about artificial intelligence in learning, it's helpful to remember the many technologies that, like graphing calculators, we once found scary but now use responsibly and ethically. Here are a few examples of how even "original work" is aided by the power of technologies (and today, many of these are being improved even further by AI).

* **Factory-made goods:** There was a time when items made by craftspeople were preferred to factory-produced items. Certainly artisanal goods are still coveted today, and there are many arts and crafts fairs to prove this point. But when it comes to refrigeration or automobiles, we have factories to thank for the mass availability of these powerful tools in our daily lives. Industry has revolutionized the availability, cost, and in some cases the quality of items we produce. We don't see machines as an inferior way to produce most products.

* **Photoshop and other graphic design programs:** Photographers and graphic artists initially thought the end was coming when these programs emerged. Instead, they embraced these tools and became even more powerful and successful in their work.

* **Computer programs:** We use word processors, spreadsheets that do calculations, website builders,

multimedia apps, internet browsers, and more. Most people don't wish we could go back to the days of typesetting, letter writing, or microfiche.

* **Online research:** Online research tools were initially thought to be less reliable than research published in books by reputable publishers, but today most academics rely heavily on online academic paper collections like JSTOR or PubMed. Certainly, tools like Wikipedia and Google created the most skepticism. Yet as the internet has evolved, we've seen that even tools like these can be extremely useful for legitimate research. As with ChatGPT, it is on the person doing the research to vet the sources and reported data.

* **Citation generators:** There was a time when you had to create all your citations from scratch and even include footnotes by using a ruler and a typewriter to create the right kind of citation notes and bibliography. Today, every college has a tool students can use to generate mostly accurate, formatted citations.

* **Spell check and grammar check:** Naturally, the goal for any paper is readable text, not proving that you know how to spell and punctuate. These tools save everyone headaches and turn writers into more proficient copyeditors of their own work. What a gift!

As a writing coach for the last several decades, I get why people who find writing intimidating see a GPT as a relief and support! Its ability to provide starter text (that initial burst of writing that relieves the screen of the empty page and blinking cursor) is invaluable. Think of it this way: while I do have writing skills, I'm as intimidated by visual design as many people are by writing. If I had to figure out color schemes or proportions on my own, I wouldn't know where to begin. But I need to use graphics when, say, creating social media posts for my business, and so for that, I rely daily on graphic design apps. I don't think twice about the fact that I didn't draw the images or develop the color palette myself. Rather, I use these apps to put together images that do the tasks I need them to do, using what skills I do have to decide what I like and don't like. That said, when it comes to brand images and professional materials that are more significant than social media posts—like Brave Writer's products, website, and online classroom—I hire a skilled graphic designer. There's no amount of "help" from an app that will give me the design eye that a professional designer can give to the visuals we need. Of course, the designers I hire also rely on graphic design apps, but their skills allow them to use those tools at a level I can't come close to approaching.

Does a GPT offer help for people who struggle with original writing in the same way graphic design apps offer help to those of us with less design skill? I was chatting the other day with my friend Mike who is a trained nurse. His skills are in the arena of keeping people alive. Mike is a veritable encyclopedia of medical knowledge far above anything I have learned as a nonmedical professional. When he was asked to write a letter of recommendation for a friend who was applying to medical school, he felt a little panicked. He hadn't ever written a letter like that and wasn't sure what a recommendation letter should contain. In point of fact, he was as uncomfortable with writing as I would be with trying to determine what medical intervention I need for an injury or illness. Not being comfortable with writing is not a crime, sin, or proof of being poorly educated. We all have our strengths and places we can use additional support.

A friend recommended that he open ChatGPT to see if it could help him write a recommendation letter. Sure enough, Mike provided the prompt, entering the details he wanted to highlight about his friend and asking the GPT to compose a letter of recommendation for medical school using those details. What he received back astonished him! The cadence, organization, and smooth language felt like a miracle. He edited the details that the GPT had misunderstood and added a few personal flourishes. He sent it on to the medical school with confidence that he had met the requirements. This kind of assist makes the GPT a revolution in writing.

But notice that the GPT couldn't speak to all the wonderful accomplishments that made my friend's colleague worthy of a recommendation letter (at least not without hallucinating). Even when a GPT can give us fluent language in the right format, it can't do our thinking for us. The content will only be as good as the prompts and inputs we give it. As students enter this brave new world of language generation, it's important that they protect their right to inventive thinking or having their own opinions. In a world where a GPT can create humanlike speech, will our students abdicate the responsibility to put their *own* thoughts into their *own* words? Will they lose the power of thinking that writing clarifies and enhances?

I recall a similar panic about the internet back in the 1990s. Adults raised the alarm: Students would purchase essays online! Students would be able to plagiarize other people's writing rather than crafting their own! Indeed, those predictions came to pass—but not for everyone. When a student doesn't value the class or learning, they will always be tempted to find a shortcut. Remember my story at the start of this book about my lawyer friend who'd paid his roommate to write his history papers? Even in the 1950s, students were finding ways not to write when they didn't want to put in the work. The goal can't be to catch kids in the act of cheating. Rather, we have to ask the harder question: What makes a student *value* what they're learning enough that they *want* to put their own thinking and effort into the tasks the teachers and professors assign? We must reform how we think about teaching and learning, not just police our students for using widely available technology.

The entire point of this book is that writing is not merely a set of mechanical skills to master. The day has come when spelling and punctuation are no longer the key markers of being an educated person. Not only that, the act of writing itself *teaches*. What if we had students who thought to themselves: *I need a minute to write about what I'm thinking so I have more clarity*? Writing is a key way that we gain access to our own minds—how we think about what we think. A GPT is only one of the revolutionary writing tools that some universities are finding ways to embrace in their courses. Other student-generated projects that are changing the landscape of academic writing include composing a script for a short video, giving an oral presentation, or using multimedia tools to teach about a concept to the class. If we focus exclusively on how to gatekeep the role of AI in our student's academic performance, we will miss the transformational moment happening right now in higher education.

I found it fascinating, for instance, that Dr. Cohen is experimenting with using AI combined with visual media for some of his class assignments. In one assignment, his students are instructed to produce short videos that analyze the principles of responsible and ethical AI. Dr. Cohen told me that he knows his students will use a GPT to create some of the content. Because he is asking them to create videos, the students find that a GPT is limited in how much help it can offer. Students must translate the content the GPT generates into film scripts that are then matched with corresponding visuals. In some cases, they can even use AI editing tools to support the film production. All of it requires a student to plan the story they want to tell, decide how they want to tell it and in what sequence, choose powerful visuals to go with the text, and edit it all into a smooth, interesting video. That's some high-level writing and thinking right there!

These student videos get uploaded to YouTube. As it turns out, college kids care more about the number of views their films get than even their grades. I've seen one of these videos and was astonished at how clever, funny, well-researched, and insightful it was! The crafting of that piece of film required every writing skill we've discussed in this book and was a far more rigorous bit of homework than slogging out a tedious essay for a one-professor audience. Even with the aid of a GPT and AI film editing tools, only a skilled user could have created the resulting cinematic deep dive into the topic. A critical lesson we may learn from the era of AI is that students are ready for a more substantive challenge than writing flat-footed essays to demonstrate their knowledge. As writing becomes a more rudimentary skill due to the rise of AI, professors and teachers will have to reinvent the kinds of assignments they expect of their students—projects that integrate a variety of modes of expression, not just a typed paper. A thoughtful video essay integrates writing, visual media, and possibly AI tools to complete the project. The result? A far more satisfying investigation into the topic at hand.

One college student I met at the University of Cincinnati blew my mind with how he had been using ChatGPT. He took daily walks in nature that lasted an hour or two at a time, speaking into his phone to record his thoughts on all topics— a kind of "freethinking" exercise similar to freewriting. The phone transcribed his words, which he uploaded to ChatGPT. Over the course of several months, he then used ChatGPT to dig through those thoughts for ideas he had overlooked, create bulleted lists of recurring themes, and even get suggestions for further exploration based on how he processes his own ideas. He said this rich experience of discovery had improved how well he performed in his software development major, because it helped him understand his own thinking at this other level. If we approach AI as a tool rather than just as a mechanism by which people cheat, we may unlock uses we haven't even considered yet!

The best role for a GPT in my mind is to use it like a virtual writing coach and as a source of starter text when we find the blank screen a bit intimidating. (Remember to vet any information it gives, though, since 15 to 20 percent of the results can be hallucinations.) AI can never do our thinking for us, but it can help us over the hurdle of just *starting.* That starter text is something to react to—we can "write back" in the same way we might "text back" or pop off with a social media comment in reaction to someone else's comment.

To preserve the power of original thinking, I suggest two key practices in the age of AI.

1. **Continue to hold big juicy conversations with students.**

   * **For parents,** this means that you deliberately discuss provocative ideas with your kids without being dogmatic propagandists for your own viewpoint. Allow the conversation to ramble, to include both logical and illogical ideas, to engage in exploration of ideas more than persuasion to your viewpoint. The more your kids learn to get comfortable talking about what they want to know and how they think, the better they'll be at guarding their original ideas and writing voice. They will *want* to include their own way of expressing themselves in their writing, even if they use a GPT as a tool for writing.

   * **For teachers,** this may mean you shift some of your assessment tools to oral presentations and tests. Presentations require a student to put whatever they've learned into their own words and to express them in front of an audience (even if it is an audience of one—you). If they use a GPT to help them find language and ideas, they will still have to know that information well enough to say it to a teacher or to an audience of students, fielding questions for clarity at the end.

European students and American graduate students are used to oral exams and orally defending their writing. This may be a moment in education where we pivot to include more opportunities for students to *speak* about what they're learning rather than only writing about it. One colleague at Xavier University told me that he invites his students to come to his office to talk about their papers after they write them. The conversation reveals how well the student knows what they put into their paper. Naturally, in large lecture hall classes, these options may not work as well; this is where labs and discussion sections are essential.

2. **Encourage timed writing.**
   * **At home,** freewrite as a family. Set aside time to handwrite (or type) freely with no agenda. Help students get comfortable forming their own ideas in their own words with their own hands. The more someone feels comfortable with writing their own thoughts, the more likely it is that they will be able to use a GPT in a skillful way. A regular freewriting practice helps individuals know their own thoughts first in their own vocabulary. Once they have a good grasp of what they think about a topic, they will be better at providing the prompts to a GPT, should they choose to use one, and they'll be better editors too.

  * **At school,** use in-class timed writing to help
    students get used to taking dictation from their
    own minds. Some of this writing should not
    be graded. Some teachers I know keep the in-
    class writing instead of returning it to the stu-
    dents, as a reference for the papers students write
    at home (a way to compare syntax and writing
    style). In addition to freewriting, teachers can
    also ask students to make lists, to write two sides
    of an issue, and to define terms that are relevant
    to the coursework and more. In-class writing
    can also be collaborative—discussing a topic in a
    group and writing a summary of the group's
    ideas.

RESPONSIBLE AND ETHICAL USES FOR AI

Naturally, there are legitimate concerns about AI beyond the
issue of cheating on school assignments. Should these programs train on the open internet without regard for copyright? (Several news outlets, publishing houses, and authors
have filed lawsuits related to this very question.) What motivation will anyone have to create original online content if it's
merely going to be scraped for AI without any credit or
link back to the creator? Would we be better served if GPTs
provided the top five links to their sources, as some GPTs are
starting to do? Computer programmers say that the more a
GPT trains on GPT-generated content, the more the technology erodes its own ability to sound as natural as a human
writing voice; will we run into a tipping point where there is

too much AI-generated content online, and how will that impact the output of these language-based tools?

As of this writing, these questions are not yet answered.
That said, AI is almost certainly here to stay, no matter what
anyone feels about it, and it has the potential to be an incredi-
bly powerful tool if it is used responsibly and ethically. In the
era of AI, the superpower we want to cultivate in our students
is the integrity to take full responsibility for vetting any AI-
assisted writing they create for accuracy, while knowing their
own point of view well enough to represent and defend it. To
me, this is an incredible opportunity to teach our kids the
importance of critical thinking, tracking down sources, and
understanding the role of experts in any field. Additionally,
once kids get the hang of interacting with these GPT tools,
they may find that their writing actually improves. The moment a student is most interested in improving their writing is
right while they're writing. A GPT offers students a chance to
get starter text, to upload and improve their own drafts, and to
edit the copy a GPT creates. In those spaces, a student is applying their analytical skills to the writing, which in turn re-
fines how they express themselves.

Here are a few ways I think AI helps us in the world of
writing.

* For those people who are endlessly tormented by
  the blank page and blinking cursor, how wonderful
  is it that you can grab starter text from AI?

* To use ChatGPT or one of its similar language generators, the user has to get better and better at issuing prompts. The writing you get back is only as

good as the precise, nuanced questions you pose. This, in itself, is an invaluable writing skill!

* Students have to vet what they learn from ChatGPT. They must understand the subject area about which they are writing well enough to see and correct any AI hallucinations. They also have to be able to modify what the program generates to suit the exact parameters of the assignment.

* ChatGPT can provide models of common writing formats; offer real-time corrections to spelling, punctuation, and grammar; and provide counterarguments to consider in order for a paper to be strengthened. The repetition of these formats and edits conditions the student to be more fluent in their writing skills. They're being instructed by a depersonalized program and are less likely to suffer the self-esteem hit that most writing instruction seems to guarantee.

* ChatGPT will save so much time. This is a feature we forget about, but it's an essential one. Whether providing a travel plan to visit Boston for the weekend or helping someone craft an application for a job, ChatGPT provides clear, intelligible language that addresses the prompt directly and immediately.

How else can AI help us in the world of education? For a little assistance with brainstorming, I asked ChatGPT to provide ten tips, and here they are, as written!

ChatGPT can be utilized for various academic purposes, including:

1. **Research Assistance:** ChatGPT can help researchers find relevant papers, summarize research articles, and provide insights into specific topics.
2. **Writing Assistance:** Students and researchers can use ChatGPT for brainstorming ideas, outlining essays, and generating drafts for academic papers.
3. **Language Learning:** ChatGPT can assist language learners in practicing writing and speaking skills through conversation and feedback.
4. **Tutoring and Education:** ChatGPT can serve as a virtual tutor, providing explanations, answering questions, and offering interactive lessons on a wide range of subjects.
5. **Data Analysis and Interpretation:** ChatGPT can help analyze data, interpret statistical results, and provide insights into complex datasets.
6. **Literature Review:** ChatGPT can assist in conducting literature reviews by summarizing key findings, identifying gaps in research, and generating annotated bibliographies.
7. **Programming Assistance:** ChatGPT can provide guidance and support for programming tasks, debugging code, and explaining programming concepts.
8. **Ethical Considerations and Debates:** ChatGPT can engage in discussions about ethical

issues in various fields, helping students and researchers explore different perspectives and arguments.

9. **Simulation and Modeling:** ChatGPT can assist in creating simulations and models, explaining mathematical concepts, and solving equations.

10. **Collaborative Projects:** ChatGPT can facilitate collaboration among students and researchers by providing a platform for brainstorming ideas, sharing resources, and coordinating tasks.

These are just a few examples of how ChatGPT can be used in academic settings. Its versatility and ability to generate humanlike text make it a valuable tool for various educational and research purposes. However, it's essential to use ChatGPT responsibly and critically evaluate its outputs, especially in academic contexts where accuracy and rigor are crucial.

Look at that—even ChatGPT advocates using AI in a responsible and ethical way. The key lesson I would love you to take away from this section of the book is that it's essential to teach your kids what it means to be responsible and ethical with AI.

Dr. Kelly Cohen puts the task of defining responsible, ethical artificial intelligence on his college students. His belief is that if students wrestle with the implications of misuse, they are more likely to use AI to enhance their education, rather than letting it take over their education. A similar task can be done with kids of any age at home. The place to begin is to bring up the philosophical concept called "ethics." What are ethics? And where do they originate? (Here's a quick definition provided by ChatGPT itself: "Ethics refers to the moral principles and values that guide individuals or groups in determining what is right or wrong, good or bad, and just or unjust.")

When Dr. Cohen and I discussed ethics, he was quick to point to the golden rule—namely, that any technology we create ought to be harnessed in ways that don't cause harm. The goal is for everyone to use AI in a way that benefits not just themselves but others as well. Dr. Cohen and his cohort of academics want to create a world in which AI usage follows guidelines related to privacy and security, transparency, accountability, fairness, reliability, and safety.

Today's thought leaders are putting effort into defining what the guidelines will be. The European Union is already establishing protocols to manage the impact of AI in all sectors—education, politics, science, and more. The United States is sure to follow. As Dr. Cohen expressed it to me, when the Wright brothers invented an airplane, there were no regulations to safeguard the public. Those came after the revolution of flight. In a similar way, the future of artificial intelligence must include guardrails so that it can be the amazing tool it is intended to be.

YOUR WRITING ASSIGNMENT

Open a large language model of your choice—ChatGPT, Gemini, or whatever new one has sprung onto the scene since the time of this writing. Play around with it. Get comfortable issuing prompts and imagine how it might be useful as a student. Here are a few starter prompts that might be fun to explore.

General knowledge:
» Tell me a fun fact about space.
» What's the difference between an alligator and a crocodile?

Educational:
» What is ChatGPT?
» Explain the Pythagorean theorem.

Creativity and fun:
» Suggest some unique party themes for a birthday party.
» What can I do on a rainy day with three kids?

Travel and adventure:
» What are some must-sees in Paris?
» Which bungee jumping sites in [place] are both safe and popular?

|||||||||||||||||||||||||

From Struggle to Bravery

There's no subject that lays bare the soul of the student like writing. Writing is the one subject in your academic life where you roll over on your back, expose your soft belly, and hope no one attacks you. Because it's so exposing, millions of grown-ups who have had ample education still find writing a little tricky or daunting. The rise of artificial intelligence to take that burden off of our hands is not surprising. Everyone wants a boost—a way to face the blank page with confidence, without terror. Your children feel this even more keenly.

Over the course of reading this book, I hope you've stuffed your tool kit with an abundance of new tactics for releasing the writer within your child. It helps to remember that struggle means pain, and pain ought to be taken seriously. We wouldn't shame or blame a child for twisting an ankle or busting an arm while playing on a playground. In the same way, we can't blame a child who misspells a word or misuses an apostrophe or cries that their hand hurts when writing. When your child struggles with writing, it means that the resources they need to feel successful are out of reach. Your task, as the caring adult in your young writer's life, is to be the bridge from their pain to their ease and success. You get to go on that journey, and through it, you'll get to know your child in brand-new, wonderful ways.

One of the pleasures of writing this book was paging through the writings my five kids did as they grew up during the seventeen years I homeschooled them. I was tickled by their vocabulary, in awe of their childlike perceptions of the world, touched by their sentiments, and surprised by how many facts they acquired as young people. I found dozens and dozens of pages filled with writing of all kinds. I discovered silly limericks, fan fiction, a lengthy novella all marked up in red-pen edits they'd made, narratives about art and nature, and reports about the Chinese New Year, India, Pablo Picasso, Martin Luther King Jr, fashion, and Pokémon. One of my kids wrote a poem to explore what it might feel like to rely on a wheelchair to get around. Another wrote their own screenplay for the Epic of Gilgamesh. All of them wrote a lot online. Several of them made international friends through online discussion boards (and eventually met them when they traveled to their countries).

There were scores of freewrites. Several released anger about being asked to write while it was still difficult. Many pieces were freewheeling looks at the thoughts a child was having that day. A few were clever and super silly. My favorite funny freewrite was written by Noah, my oldest, when he was twelve. We went on a walk in our neighborhood in the dead of winter. I asked each child to pick a color to observe. He picked orange. When we returned home, he wrote an interview with the color orange, asking how it felt to be completely ignored in an entire season of the year. It was hilarious!

When I look at it all now, it's like reading a portrait of the inner life of each of my children. Their writing is far more accurate in showing me who they were at each age and stage of life than any school picture. There's something so disarming about reading a child's writing at five, then nine, then fourteen, and then eighteen, as they leave for college. This record of their developing personalities, tastes, and intellects is precious to me. That journey was more meaningful than any photo album I have. It was like paging through snapshots of their minds, brimming with glimpses of the amazing people they would become. My oldest and youngest both majored in linguistics. One of my kids went to law school. My son who struggled with dysgraphia wound up studying at a Great Books program in college and has an active Substack. And Johannah, whose writing I have featured at times in this book, continues to write evocatively as she studies to be a licensed therapist.

In each of their lives, writing is available as a tool, as a gift, as a means of knowing themselves and others. The goal of writing instruction isn't necessarily to teach students to become the published author of a Great American Novel. Rather, I'd love to see kids grow up feeling like they *want* to write their own thoughts in their own words, whether it be wedding vows or a eulogy for a family member. I hope to see a generation of adults treat writing as a sacred trust—the opportunity to give our children the gift of self-knowledge and the privilege of being read for who they are. Each child deserves to write and be read. I hope this book has given you the courage to be that kind, supportive adult in your child's writing life. Your kids ought to know that they have the right to write, now, no matter how skillfully they handwrite, spell, or punctuate—for themselves first, and for others when they are ready.

RESOURCES

IIIIIIIIIIIIIIIIIIIIIII

I f you're looking for tools to help you teach your kids writing—as a home educator, as a parent who wants to augment what your kids are learning in school, or as a teacher looking for a fresh approach to writing—here are some resources I recommend.

BRAVE WRITER

My company, Brave Writer, has taught nearly a million children over the last twenty-five years, through our online writing classes and through *Growing Brave Writers*, the curriculum that teaches all the processes that students need to become proficient writers. We teach kids *how* to write, rather than just describing an endless series of writing formats. Our track record includes students who've gone on to win awards for their writing, to be published, to major in English, journalism, and creative writing. They've started blogs and media companies.

They've earned advanced degrees, have had their books published, and have worked in nearly every field, from engineering to psychology. What we hear back the most is that by the time our students get to college, they feel well prepared for that academic journey. Why? Because they know how to *think*, and then how to put those thoughts into writing. My hope is that we can continue to transform how writing is taught in this country so that we don't keep damaging scores of children.

Please check our website (bravewriter.com) and my social media and YouTube channel for even more programs and resources. I also have a well-loved podcast called *Brave Writer* that may be a wonderful support to your leadership in your child's life.

BOOKS

My first book, *The Brave Learner*, lays a foundation for how to create the context for kids to thrive academically and personally.

My second book, *Raising Critical Thinkers*, is designed to support you in your goals of building skillful thinkers who can express themselves well both in writing and orally. My companion workbook, *Becoming a Critical Thinker*, gives your students (ages twelve to eighteen) a chance to work through activities that expand how they analyze, understand, and examine ideas and texts. It's a fabulous complement to this book!

ACKNOWLEDGMENTS

||||||||||||||||||||||||||||||||||||||||||

Writing a book about writing is such a meta experience. My own journey as a writer kept flashing before my mind's eye as I thanked each person who had a hand in my writing development. I could almost hear the voices of those who have been most valuable in that growth as both a published author and a writing coach.

Thanks first to my agent and editors. Thank you, Rita Rosenkranz, for always advocating for my work and supporting me as I do it. I love our relationship and am grateful for your guidance. Thank you to Joanna Ng for your wise support in helping me launch my book writing career. Thank you, Lauren O'Neal, for taking up the next leg of that journey. Lauren, you offered such skillful edits. What a treat to work with you!

The two most important professional writers and educators who have shaped me are the late Pat Schneider and the great Dr. Peter Elbow. These two pioneers collaborated at University of Massachusetts in Amherst. *Writing Alone and with Others* and *Writing with Power* have given me such good ground to grow in. I offer them to you, dear reader, as tools for enhancing your skills with your kids. Peter: thank you for being my mentor and friend all these years. I'm honored and grateful.

These additional writers have had a profound impact on me too: E. M. Forster, Anne Lamott, Natalie Goldberg, William Zinsser, and Susan Goldsmith Wooldridge.

My entire team at Brave Writer is tireless in their dedication to making writing a pleasant and empowering experience for our students. In addition to Cindy, Dawn, and Kirsten, who were mentioned in the dedication, I am proud to work alongside other core staff members: Jeannette Hall, Diana Allor, and Rebecca Pickens. The teaching staff provides the most loving, empowering guidance ever to our writing students. They inspire me every day with their kindness and commitment!

Melissa Wiley, my cohost on the *Brave Writer* podcast, is one of my favorite writing colleagues and friends. Her early friendship as we developed our writing careers has been a continuous source of inspiration and joy for nearly three decades!

A special shout-out to my kids, whose writing has always brought me delight and inspiration: Noah, Johannah, Jacob, Liam, and Caitrin. I am grateful to Jon, my ex-husband, for his contributions to my growth as a writer too. How many long, helpful conversations did we share? How many of his college composition books did I plunder? Too many to count.

Thanks to the person who keeps me going every day: Jim Schaefer.

I am most indebted to my mother—Karen O'Connor. She's the author of seventy-two books with more than two million copies sold in her lifetime. Mom, thank you for all the ways that you have shown me the value and power of my writing voice. I learned from you: I write, therefore I am. I love you. May that gift be extended even further through these pages to all the wonderful parents and teachers who are reading along.

NOTES

||||||||||||

INTRODUCTION

xx   four freewrites of fifteen minutes each: Shilagh A. Mirgain and Janice Singles, "Therapeutic Journaling," VA Office of Patient Centered Care and Cultural Transformation, 2016, https://www.va.gov/WHOLEHEALTHLIBRARY/docs/Therapeutic-Journaling.pdf.

xxi   my writing mentor, Dr. Peter Elbow: Peter Elbow, "Teaching Thinking by Teaching Writing," *Change* 15, no. 6 (1983): 37–40, https://doi.org/10.1080/00091383.1983.10570005.

CHAPTER 1: WRITING IS HARD

13   Nineteenth-century British educator: Charlotte M. Mason, *Home Education* (Carol Stream, IL: Tyndale House, 1989), 247.

CHAPTER 4: HEALING THE DAMAGED WRITER IN YOU

54   When teaching anyone to write: Pat Schneider, *Writing Alone and with Others* (New York: Oxford University Press, 2003), 191.

56 the field of occupational therapy: Patricia Oetter, Eileen W. Richter, and Sheila M. Frick, *M. O. R. E.: Integrating the Mouth with Sensory and Postural Functions* (Hugo, MN: PDP Press, 1993).

CHAPTER 5: GOOD WRITING IS SURPRISING WRITING

63 **"Shelby Strother told me a long time ago":** Gene Wojciechowski, "An Interview with Gene Wojciechowski," interview by Steve Marantz, SteveMarantz.com, September 22, 2017.

63 **"If you love watching sweat dry":** Gene Wojciechowski, "Bruins' Stingy D Turns Tigers into Cats," ESPN.com, April 2, 2006, https://www.espn.com/espn/columns/story?columnist=wojciechowski_gene&id=2393709.

64 **"The Bruins don't simply play defense":** Wojciechowski, "Bruins' Stingy D."

64 **"'Where's Papa going with that ax?'":** E. B. White, *Charlotte's Web* (New York: Harper, 1952), 1.

CHAPTER 9: LET YOUR KIDS CLEAN UP THEIR MESSY WRITING

151 **C. H. Knoblauch and Lil Brannon:** Arlene Silberman, *Growing Up Writing: Teaching Children to Write, Think, and Learn* (New York: Times Books, 1989), 55.

152 **One of the staggering findings:** C. H. Knoblauch and Lil Brannon, "Teacher Commentary on Student Writing: The State of the Art," *Freshman English News* 10, no. 2 (Fall 1981), 1–4, http://www.jstor.org/stable/43518564.

152 **responsive writing feedback:** Nancy Sommers, "Responding to Student Writing," *College Composition and Communication* 33, no. 2 (May 1982), 155, https://doi.org/10.2307/357622.

CHAPTER 10: HOW WRITERS GROW NATURALLY

212 **This kind of writing activity:** Rachel Kadish, "The Most Important Writing Exercise I've Ever Assigned," *The New York Times*, February 18, 2024, https://www.nytimes.com/2024/02/18/opinion/radical-empathy-fiction.html.

CHAPTER 11: SPELLING, PUNCTUATION, AND GRAMMAR

221 **memorizing words in a list:** Rebecca Rymer and Cheri Williams, "'Wasn't That a Spelling Word?': Spelling Instruction and Young Children's Writing," *Language Arts* 77, no. 3 (January 2000), 241–49, http://www.jstor.org/stable/41483059.

222 **five thousand French adults:** Joe Hernandez, "A Massive Dictation Event Takes over the Iconic Champs-Élysées in Paris," NPR, June 5, 2023, www.npr.org/2023/06/05/1180134832/champs-elysees-paris -giant-dictation.

CHAPTER 12: ARTIFICIAL INTELLIGENCE AND WRITING

233 **"learn[ing] patterns and relationships":** Harry Guinness, "How Does ChatGPT Work?," Zapier, February 27, 2023, https://zapier.com/blog /how-does-chatgpt-work/.

234 **a high-profile legal case:** Associated Press, "Michael Cohen Says He Unwittingly Sent AI-Generated Fake Legal Cases to His Attorney," National Public Radio, December 30, 2023, https://www.npr.org /2023/12/30/1222273745/michael-cohen-ai-fake-legal-cases.

234 **director of the AI Biolab:** Kelly Cohen, "A Deep Dive into AI with Dr. Kelly Cohen," interview by Julie Bogart, *Brave Writer*, April 10, 2024, https://blog.bravewriter.com/2024/04/10/podcast-dive-into-ai -dr-kelly-cohen/.

235 **about 15 to 20 percent:** Maryna Bilan, "Hallucinations in LLMs: What You Need to Know before Integration," Master of Code Global, July 14, 2023, https://masterofcode.com/blog/hallucinations-in-llms -what-you-need-to-know-before-integration.

235 **In February 2024:** Kim Leoffler, "UNG Student on Academic Probation for Alleged AI-Use Partners with Grammarly," FOX 5 Atlanta, March 8, 2024, www.fox5atlanta.com/news/georgia-ung -grammarly-ai-cheating-plagiarism-partnership.

236 **"A more comprehensive solution":** Lauren Coffey, "Professors Cautious of Tools to Detect AI-Generated Writing," *Inside Higher Ed*, February 9, 2024, https://www.insidehighered.com/news/tech-in-

novation/artificial-intelligence/2024/02/09/professors-proceed-caution-using-ai.

236 **In Dr. Kelly Cohen's engineering classes:** Cohen, "A Deep Dive into AI."

243 **In one assignment:** Cohen, "A Deep Dive into AI."

251 **Dr. Kelly Cohen puts the task:** Cohen, "A Deep Dive into AI."

252 **When Dr. Cohen and I:** Cohen, "A Deep Dive into AI."

252 **As Dr. Cohen expressed it:** Cohen, "A Deep Dive into AI."

INDEX

||||||||||||

III

Julie Bogart is the creator of the award-winning, innovative Brave Writer program, teaching writing and language arts to thousands of families for more than twenty-five years. Brave Writer ranked in the top ten women-owned businesses in the National Association of Women's Business Owners in 2024. Bogart is also the founder of Brave Learner Home, a 17,000-member community that supports homeschooling parents through coaching and teaching, and the host of the popular *Brave Writer* podcast. She holds a BA from UCLA and an MA from Xavier University, where she's taught as an adjunct professor and was awarded the prestigious Madges Award for Outstanding Contribution to Society. Bogart has five adult kids, whom she homeschooled for seventeen years, and three delightful grandchildren. Her other books include *The Brave Learner, Raising Critical Thinkers, and Becoming a Critical Thinker.* You can follow her on Instagram @juliebravewriter.